GREAT MYSTERIES

Evolution

OPPOSING VIEWPOINTS®

Look for these and other exciting *Great Mysteries: Opposing Viewpoints* books:

GREAT MYSTERIES

Evolution

OPPOSING VIEWPOINTS®

by Marilyn Bailey

Greenhaven Press, Inc.   P.O. Box 289009, San Diego, California 92198-0009

Library of Congress Cataloging-in-Publication Data

Bailey, Marilyn
    Evolution: opposing viewpoints / by Marilyn Bailey.
      p. cm. — (Great mysteries)
    Includes bibliographical references and index.
    Summary: Presents opposing views of experts on the origins of earth and its creatures. Explores the Bible story, Darwinian theories, fossils, and carbon-dating techniques.
    ISBN 0-89908-078-2 (lib. bdg.)
    1. Evolution—Juvenile literature. [1. Evolution] I. Title.
II. Series: Great mysteries (Saint Paul, Minn.)
QH367.1.B35 1990
757—dc20   90-35611
                                                                  CIP
                                                                  AC

For Robert, who first made this book possible, then made it practical, with gratitude for the patience and caring.
For John, Bob, Reneé, and William, for their encouragement in my evolution as a person and a writer, with love.
With special thanks to Jerald A. Larson, M.A., for sharing his enthusiasm for evolution with me.

Contents

Introduction

This book is written for the curious—those who want to explore the mysteries that are everywhere. To be human is to be constantly surrounded by wonderment. How do birds fly? Are ghosts real? Can animals and people communicate? Was King Arthur a real person or a myth? Why did Amelia Earhart disappear? Did history really happen the way we think it did? Where did the world come from? Where is it going?

Great Mysteries: Opposing Viewpoints books are intended to offer the reader an opportunity to explore some of the many mysteries that both trouble and intrigue us. For the span of each book, we want the reader to feel that he or she is a scientist investigating the extinction of the dinosaurs, an archaeologist searching for clues to the origin of the great Egyptian pyramids, a psychic detective testing the existence of ESP.

One thing all mysteries have in common is that there is no ready answer. Often there are *many* answers but none on which even the majority of authorities agrees. *Great Mysteries: Opposing Viewpoints* books introduce the intriguing views of the experts, allowing the reader to participate in their explorations, their theories, and their disagreements as they try to explain the mysteries of our world.

But most readers won't want to stop here. These *Great Mysteries: Opposing Viewpoints* aim to stimulate the reader's curiosity. Although truth is often impossible to discover, the search is fascinating. It is up to the reader to examine the evidence, to decide whether the answer is there—or to explore further.

"Penetrating so many secrets, we cease to believe in the unknowable. But there it sits nevertheless, calmly licking its chops."

H.L. Mencken, American essayist

One

What Is Evolution?

*The sky was large and very clear. It was empty;
there were no stars and no moon; only a tree stood
in the air, and there was wind. This tree fed on the
atmosphere and ants lived on it. Wind, tree, ants,
and atmosphere were controlled by the power of
the Word. But the Word was not something that
could be seen. It was a force that enabled one
thing to create another.*
—A myth of the Wapangwa people of Tanzania,
South Africa.

For thousands of years, people have made up stories about the world and how it and the creatures
living in it came to be. Before there was science,
humans watched the lights in the sky and the animals on the earth and wondered about them. They
made up myths, like the one above, to explain their
world.

As people observed the sky, the plants, the animals, the land, and the climate, they began to see
the regular happenings of nature. They began to
draw some conclusions about what nature's patterns
mean. They observed clues to the ways things came
to be as they are.

In the late nineteenth century, Charles Darwin, a
methodical, dedicated, and astute observer of na-

(Opposite page) Charles
Darwin changed history
when he formulated the
theory of evolution by natural
selection. He devoted his life
to conducting research to
support his theory.

"First there was the great cosmic egg. Inside the egg was chaos, and floating in chaos was P'an Ku, the Undeveloped, the divine embryo. And P'an Ku burst out of the egg, four times larger than any man today, with a hammer and chisel in his hand with which he fashioned the world."

Third century Chinese myth

"Na Arean sat alone in space as a cloud that floats in nothingness. He slept not, for there was no sleep; he hungered not, for as yet there was no hunger. So he remained for a great while, until a thought came to his mind. He said to himself, 'I will make a thing.'"

Maianan myth from the Gilbert Islands

ture, developed the involved idea that has become known as the theory of evolution. This theory has been wildly controversial but also has become widely accepted as a likely explanation for why the world and its plants and animals are as they are today.

What Is the Theory of Evolution?

The word *evolution* means slow or gradual change. Scientists use the term *theory of evolution* to identify their thinking of how life came about. The theory says that all life on earth began from a *primordial,* or ancient, cell and changed or evolved to become every kind of living thing on earth. The theory of evolution says that existing *species*, or kinds, of plants and animals have developed from previously existing species through a gradual process of change. Scientists believe that the primordial cell was a simple form of life, much like bacteria. That simple cell evolved into multi-celled *organisms,* living things, both animals and plants. The organisms kept evolving into more and more complicated life forms, including humans.

A theory is more than an idea or a guess. It is a conclusion drawn after accumulation of much evidence. A theory can never be proved true. But it must contain definite enough ideas so that it can be proved wrong or it does not qualify as a theory.

For instance, there is not enough evidence to absolutely prove that life started with simple forms and evolved to more complex ones. But so far, only traces of simple organisms have been found in Precambrian rocks, which are between six hundred million and four billion years old. If fish bones were found in Precambrian rocks, the scientific theory of evolution would be proved wrong. The fish bones would tell scientists that more complicated life lived at the same time as those simple bacteria-like organisms. That might mean that more complicated life did not evolve from simple life.

Scientists gather evidence that seems to say that something happens in a certain way. They tell other scientists their idea. Other scientists test the theory, almost as if they are playing "king of the mountain." They try to "knock the theory off the mountain" by finding evidence that the theory is not true. The more times scientists fail to prove a theory false, the more likely the theory is to be true.

When three and a half billion-year-old rocks were found in Canada and Australia in the 1950s, scientists searched for evidence of life. If they had found an oyster shell, for example, the theory of evolution would have been disproven, or at least shown to be inaccurate. But no oysters or other more complex life forms were discovered. Only simple life forms were found in those ancient rocks. Once again, evidence backed up the theory of evolution and made it more likely to be "true."

Before Evolution—Geology

Before Darwin came up with his theory that even today some people think of as outrageous, other scientists made discoveries that helped him. These discoveries were the beginning of *geology*, the science that studies the earth's crust, its physical changes, and the causes that produce such changes.

These discoveries seem so simple today that we cannot imagine a time when people did not know these things. These discoveries, which became basic laws of geology, are:

The *Principle of Horizontality*, discovered by the Danish physician Nicholas Steno in 1669. He watched sediment, such as sand or fine granules of gravel, being moved in a stream. He saw that the sediment is positioned in flat and nearly horizontal layers. Irregularities are covered and smoothed over by successive deposits of sediments.

The *Principle of Superposition*, also deduced by

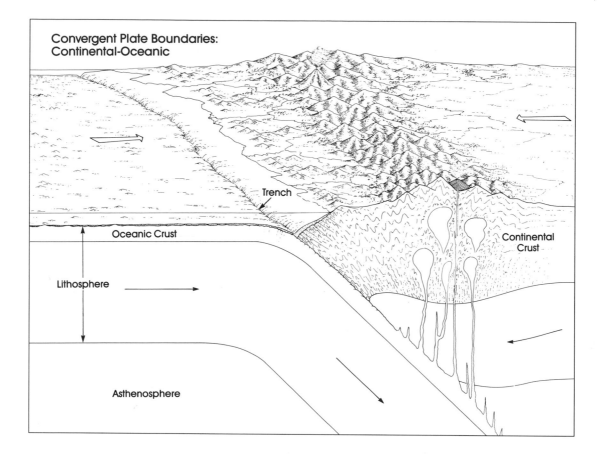

**Convergent Plate Boundaries:
Continental-Oceanic**

Trench

Oceanic Crust

Lithosphere

Asthenosphere

Continental
Crust

Today we know that tectonic activity is responsible for the restructuring of many ancient continental locations. Here, moving plates of the lithosphere are driven together by currents in the asthenosphere. Mountains form as the plates are pushed upward.

Steno: The layer on the bottom is older than the layers on top of it.

The *Principle of Uniformitarianism,* discovered by Scottish scientist James Hutton in 1788. This was one part of what he called his "Theory of the Earth." This principle says that processes of nature taking place on earth today (such as sediment being laid down horizontally) happened the same way in the past. These processes of nature are uniform, he said. They are the same natural occurrences whether they happened millions of years ago or today.

The present is the key to the past is the second part of Hutton's Theory of the Earth. This principle says that we can deduce, or figure out, what natural event happened in the past from looking at the effects of the same kind of a natural event now. For example, when scientists find a layer of lava that is millions of years old, they know the lava came from a volcano that erupted millions of years ago.

In the past, as today, scientists from many countries shared their ideas and findings. In England, Charles Lyell, a friend of Darwin's, heard about Hutton's Principle of Uniformitarianism. Lyell expanded the idea in his three-volume *Principles of Geology.* This work would be very important to Darwin.

These discoveries pointed to an old earth. In Lyell's time, the early and middle 1800s, most people, even scientists, still thought the earth was young. In 1654, a respected Irish archbishop, James Ussher, used information in the Bible to figure out that God had created Adam and Eve in 4004 B.C. Other scholars confirmed his finding, even coming up with an exact date: 9 a.m., October 26, 4004 B.C.

Even though most people accepted Ussher's views, they saw many "oddities of nature" that did not fit into the theory of a six-thousand-year-old earth. To explain these oddities, some scientists proposed the idea that great world-wide violent catastrophes caused drastic changes in the earth's surface. Such catastrophes as Noah's flood tumbled rocks about, folded them, and laid sediment in uneven layers. These great catastrophes caused the oddities, they believed.

The Journey That Changed History

When Charles Darwin set off on his five-year journey to South America on the H.M.S. *Beagle*, he, too, believed that God had created the world only a few thousand years earlier.

The *Beagle* had been commissioned by the British Navy to survey the coasts of the Straits of Magellan and of Tierra del Fuego, the large island

A volcano erupts, spewing lava into the atmosphere. Scientists know that volcanoes erupted with the same explosive force millions of years ago.

"And God made the beasts of the earth according to their kinds and the cattle according to their kind and everything that creeps upon the ground according to its kind."

Genesis 1:25

"The millions of species of animals and plants that have ever lived on the Earth all evolved from a single common ancestry by a natural process over hundreds of millions of years. Such change is beautifully revealed in the fossil record of past life."

Science writer Roy A. Gallant, *Fossils*

that forms the southernmost tip of South America. Darwin was invited to make the journey as an unpaid naturalist. Before departure, the ship's captain, Robert Fitzroy, told Darwin he was convinced beyond a doubt that Darwin's observations of plants, animals, and fossils would prove once and for all the "scientific truth of the Book of Genesis, which described how God created the world and all living things. Darwin agreed that Fitzroy was probably right," says Roy Gallant in *Charles Darwin, The Making of a Scientist*.

A deeply religious man, Darwin did not see himself as a scientist, but rather as an amateur collector. He would be going into the ministry of the Church of England when he returned home. Darwin took with him Lyell's *Principles of Geology.*

While Fitzroy did the surveying for which the journey had been set up, Darwin did his observing and collecting. "His appetite for facts was endless," Gallant writes. "His eyes and ears seldom missed anything."

Darwin made thousands of observations of how living things have adapted to their environment. Darwin collected, studied, dissected, examined with his microscope, classified, and put up specimens in bottles of preservative liquids. One member of the crew sometimes yelled at Darwin for messing up his decks with dead fish, bird skins, fossil bones, and rocks, but he fondly referred to Darwin as "our fly catcher," says Gallant.

Puzzling Fossils

At Bahía Blanca, Darwin made the first discovery that confused him, because it did not seem to agree with the Biblical "truths" he had been taught since childhood. At the foot of a cliff, he dug out a large animal head fossil he felt was related to the Rhinoceros. He found another large jaw bone that still held one tooth. When he showed the fossil to

Fitzroy, the captain said, "*obviously* the bones belonged to huge animals that . . . did not get aboard Noahs ark in time to be saved from the Flood."

Darwin did not argue. Today scientists say the skull belonged to a *Toxodon*, an animal that became extinct about two million years ago. The jaw was that of the extinct giant *Megatherium*. Darwin found seven more fossil bones of giant animals he knew did not exist in his time. Darwin marveled at how these extinct animals resembled living animals he was seeing day after day. The Toxodon looked like a South American rodent about the size of a big collie, called *capybara*. The Megatherium resembled the still-living, much smaller South American sloths. Another fossil find was a giant relative of the armadillo.

Later, after finding another large extinct animal that was similar to a llama, he saw a pattern that "screamed for attention," according to Gallant. Darwin saw that certain species lived in the same area where extinct similar species once roamed. One or two fossils of extinct animals that resembled living species might have been a matter of chance, he reasoned. But three, four, and later dozens? . . . No.

The skull of a *Nanotyrannus lancensis*. Scientists study such fossils to learn about species that became extinct millions of years ago.

A drawing depicts Noah's ark during the flood. Did God create all species of animals purportedly housed in the ark?

Why had these animals become extinct, Darwin wondered. What connection did these species of the past have with animals of the present?

Darwin also found another kind of puzzle. Fossil remains showed that horses had lived in South America millions of years ago. Why, then, were horses unknown to South Americans when the Spanish brought them there in the 1500s? Why had the horses died out?

Darwin kept looking for signs of sudden, violent changes that would be evidence of catastrophism and would explain the mysterious extinctions. But what he found showed no catastrophes.

The evidence told him that the land had formed slowly over millions of years.

Darwin often went ashore and made many long journeys over the land as Fitzroy did his surveying at sea. He saw a rich variety of life living in many kinds of environments. "Every part of the world is habitable!" he wrote. "Whether lakes of brine, or those underground ones hidden beneath volcanic mountains, or warm mineral springs, or wide expanse and depths of the ocean, or the upper regions of the atmosphere, and even the surface of perpetual snow—all support living things." He would later argue in his *Origin of the Species* that species evolved or expanded to fill empty "niches" in the environment.

Mountains of Evidence

Darwin walked hundreds of miles when the *Beagle* was off on its surveying task, making his observations and collecting species. He roamed the western coast of South America and the Pampas plain in Argentina. One challenge he set himself was to investigate the Andes Mountains. The mountain system stretches for four thousand miles, from Venezuela to the southern-most tip of South America. As Gallant says, "Darwin got a geology lesson he had not asked for. It came as a violent earthquake." He saw that the earthquake had raised the harbor at Concepcion two or three feet. The earthquake, Darwin wrote, "at once destroyed our oldest idea that Earth is the very emblem of solidity, for it moved beneath our feet like a thin crust over a fluid." He could picture continents slowly, over time, being uplifted by repeated earthquakes and volcanic eruptions. He carried his geologist's hammer up and down the Andes, finding rocks and fossils that told the history of those huge mountains.

He wrote about seeing a group of petrified trees at seven thousand feet above sea level: "I was at first so astonished I could scarcely believe the plainest evidence. . . . I had come upon a spot where . . . trees once waved their branches on the shore of the Atlantic when that ocean [now 700 miles away] came to the foot of the Andes."

As he chipped away with his hammer, he could see that a section of sea floor had risen up, dried out, and become a garden of trees. Then the land sank and was washed once again by the sea. Next it was covered, layer by layer, with sand, clay, and other sediments carried down from the land by rivers and streams. The small valleys and canyons in the mountains were wide-open pages of the fossil record. There Darwin could see that lava flows had built up at five different times. Then each was covered with sediment washed down from the land and built up again, all under the sea. At first only a

Charles Darwin spent time exploring the Andes Mountains in South America.

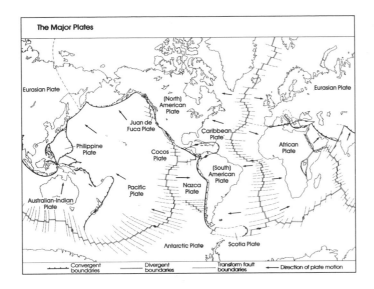

The Major Plates

A map of the major tectonic plates of the earth. The theory of plate tectonics is broadly supported by scientific research.

small ridge of land lay above water for a stretch of four thousand miles. Then gradually, bit by bit, forces within the earth pushed the ridge upward until it was fifteen thousand feet above the sea. That was when the trees, now petrified, stood on the ocean shore. Later the land rose again until finally the seven-hundred-mile-wide Pampas plain was thrust into sunlight.

Today we know from research done by the U.S. Navy during World War II that the surface of the earth is not as solid as it looks. It is made up of what scientists call *tectonic plates* that float on molten rock, much like chunks of ice float on a river. When two plates collide, their edges are forcibly pushed upward. Rocks crumble. The friction of the rocks smashing against each other makes some of the rocks so hot they melt and are folded. As the plates continue to push against each other, mountains eventually are formed. Sometimes volcanoes erupt between plates and push up the surface of the earth. The Andes Mountains, and others, were built by such tectonic activity. Darwin did not know anything about tectonic plates, but he saw the

While studying finches, Darwin theorized that better adapted finches survived a particular habitat long enough to reproduce. The trait that enabled the bird to survive is passed on to its offspring.

evidence of their activity.

"He marveled," Gallant says, "at the forces capable of crumpling and twisting the solid rock of Earth's crust as though it were paper."

Biological Treasure

Darwin found a geological treasure in the Andes. He was to find a biological treasure in the Galapagos Islands, which lie five hundred miles off the coast of Ecuador. There, Darwin found *flora* and *fauna*, or plants and animals, so spectacular that they made him question the distribution of creation.

He found twenty-six species of birds, twenty-five of which were unknown anywhere else. He found thirteen species of finches. He found giant tortoises that were found in no other place in the world. One of them measured fifty-five inches from neck to tail and weighed, Darwin guessed, about five hundred pounds.

When he later studied the finches, he found that the various species had similar bodies, built the same kind of nests, and laid the same number of the same color eggs. They looked like finches he had found in South America. But their beaks were strikingly different. Some were stubby, almost parrot-like. The finches with such beaks could crack hard nuts and crush smaller seeds. Other beaks were long and needle-like. The finches with these beaks ate soft fruits and flowers. One finch even used its beak as a tool to get at food in trees. The island on which it lived had no woodpeckers, so the finch filled that environmental niche.

Why Do Finches Differ?

"Darwin marveled over the difference in structure," Gallant says. "But he had not discovered the most remarkable thing about those birds." That discovery came to him some time after the Vice-Governor of the Galapagos told Darwin he could tell from one look on what island an animal had been caught. When Darwin later began to sort out his finches, he discovered that all finches belonging to one island had one kind of beak and were of one species, while all finches from another island had another kind of beak and belonged to another species. Darwin thought how that might have happened. In the struggle for food, one finch accidentally might have been able to crack open and live on seeds. It would have an advantage over birds who could eat only insects. In time, according to the kind of food available on each island, the finches

"The fact of evolution is as well established as anything in science, though absolute certainty has no place in the lexicon of science."

Dr. Stephen Jay Gould, *Discover* Magazine, January 1987

"The reason that most scientists accept the theory of evolution is that most scientists are unbelievers, and unbelieving materialistic men are forced to accept a materialistic, naturalistic explanation for the origin of all living things."

Institute of Creation Research's Dr. Duane T. Gish, *Evolution? The Fossils Say No!*

who could adapt to eating that food survived. Each generation of its offspring changed slightly until that species was in tune with its environment. This observation was the germ of Darwin's later theory of natural selection.

Natural Selection

Darwin's idea of natural selection has four parts:

(1) Most species produce more offspring than can survive.

(2) An individual's chances of surviving are affected by the environment in which it lives. Environment includes weather, food, a place to live, other organisms to mate with, and other plants and

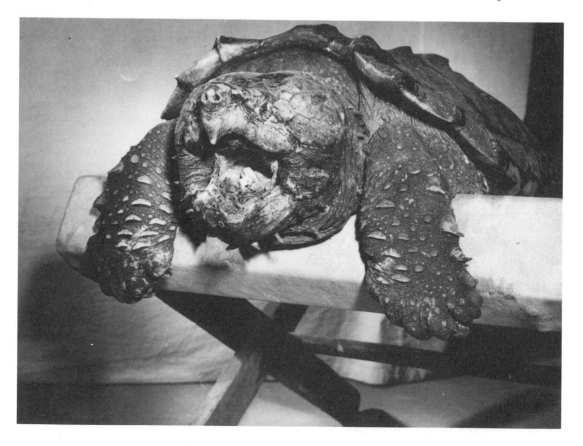

An alligator-snapping turtle is equipped with a natural lure to catch fish—a white object in the center of its lower jaw. The lure entices fish and other water animals to swim directly into the turtle's mouth, where they are devoured with a snap of the jaw. Darwin believed that traits like this enabled animals to survive harsh environments.

animals. Plants and animals that get along best in their environment have the best chance of surviving and reproducing more of their kind.

(3) Individuals vary. Some are better adapted than others to their environment and stand a better chance of surviving. Darwin did not know what caused individuals to be different. We now know that variation is caused by mutations and a "mixing up" of genes during sexual reproduction. The behavior or trait that enables organisms to survive is passed on to their young.

(4) Better adapted individuals survive long enough to reproduce, and they pass on to their offspring the characteristics that helped them survive. "So nature tends to select for survival those individuals with the 'right' instincts," Gallant says. "Individuals with the 'wrong' instincts tend to perish."

A Common Ancestor?

As Darwin thought about the varieties of finches, he imagined a time when the islands of the Galapagos had just risen out of the sea, when there was nothing but cooling lava. Then somehow land birds made their way to the islands. Their droppings contained seeds, and soon plant life arose. As plant life spread, the islands became habitable and other animals came. "As each species arrived on an island," Gallant reports, "it either perished or adjusted to conditions there, each generation of offspring changing slightly until eventually the species was in tune with its environment. Since conditions on each island were different . . . a species settling on one island would develop differently from others of its members who settled on a different island."

Those thirteen species of finches came from one ancestor, Darwin concluded. And that ancestor had come from a still more ancient ancestor. In some mysterious way, life could be traced back to but one primitive kind of being.

"The fact of evolution for which evidence is overwhelming is simply that the earth and its living organisms have evolved."

Science editor, Dennis Flanagan, *Flanagan's Version*

"We can't say that evolution has been 'explained' until we know more about the factors which determine form."

British Television science advisor Gordon Rattray Taylor, *The Great Evolution Mystery*

Darwin could no longer accept the Biblical account of God putting all species on the earth on a particular day six thousand years before. Each species was not created separately, instantaneously, as he had thought. He still believed God was the Creator, but he believed creation happened differently than it was recorded in Genesis. He believed the truth could only be found if people probed back into geological time by learning to read the fossil record.

Stormy Weather at Home

"There is no use trying," said Alice. "One *can't* believe impossible things."

"I dare say you haven't had much practice," said the Queen. "When I was your age, I always did it for half an hour a day. Why, sometimes I believed as many as six impossible things before breakfast."

—Author Lewis Carroll, *Through the Looking Glass*

The conclusions Darwin came to after his voyage could be called "impossible things to believe." The people of his day were like Alice. They would find it difficult, Darwin knew, to believe the conclusions he had reached. At that time, according to Maitland Edey and Donald C. Johanson in their book *Blueprints*, the Biblical account of creation, including Bishop Ussher's idea of a six-thousand-year-old earth, was accepted as true.

Such thinking "was the familiar, comfortable . . . fortress on which the Crown, Church, the stability of Empire, the dependability of society, and the respectability of individuals and their thinking depended on," say Edey and Johanson.

But most scientists had begun to accept the idea of an old earth. Geology, as a science, was growing. Some scientists still argued that catastrophe, not age, was responsible for how the rocks were deposited and for the kinds of fossils the rocks held.

Lava flows after a volcanic eruption. Lava originates as magma—molten material formed in the earth's crust.

But most of the arguing took place privately. Scientists read their papers about the age of earth's rocks in scientific meetings. But the subject of those papers went unnoticed by the public. The age of earth's rocks was a dull subject.

But questions about God's role as Creator were not. Such questions threatened established order. When Darwin was two years old, the poet Shelley was expelled from Oxford University because of his pamphlet *The Necessity of Atheism.* "Not one natural scientist stood up to support him, although there must have been quite a few who secretly did—if

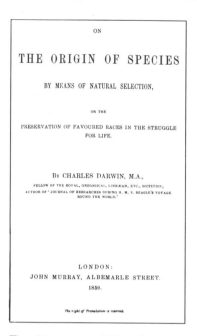

ON

THE ORIGIN OF SPECIES

BY MEANS OF NATURAL SELECTION,

OR THE

PRESERVATION OF FAVOURED RACES IN THE STRUGGLE
FOR LIFE.

By CHARLES DARWIN, M.A.,

FELLOW OF THE ROYAL, GEOLOGICAL, LINNÆAN, ETC., SOCIETIES;
AUTHOR OF 'JOURNAL OF RESEARCHES DURING H. M. S. BEAGLE'S VOYAGE
ROUND THE WORLD.'

LONDON:
JOHN MURRAY, ALBEMARLE STREET.
1859.

The right of Translation is reserved.

The title page of *The Origin of Species* by Charles Darwin. Published in 1859, the book raised a storm of controversy.

atheism meant not believing in a literal account of Creation," Edey and Johanson report. Darwin's grandfather, Erasmas Darwin, had also had questions about a different sort of creation, but he had "cautiously concealed them in a long poem, 'The Temple of Nature.'"

No wonder Darwin was concerned that his theory would make people angry. He risked being made a social outcast and being labeled a fool. Yet he wanted "to take a place" among the leading scientists of his day. He was twenty-five years old when he returned from his voyage on the *Beagle*. He was fifty years old when his book, *The Origin of Species*, was published.

As he wrote his book, he tried to anticipate and answer every argument that might arise. His friend Lyell was against Darwin's ideas about species changes. Nevertheless, he urged Darwin to hurry. He warned him that if he did not publish his views, someone else would think of them and get the credit.

Alfred Russel Wallace

It almost happened. A young naturalist, Alfred Russel Wallace, who had been exploring the East Indies, wrote to Darwin expressing views similar to his. Wallace, too, was worried about making a fool of himself. He asked Darwin to show the ideas to Lyell if Darwin thought them "worthy." Darwin wrote Wallace, praising his ideas, but he wondered how he could honorably publish his own sketch now. He feared others might think he stole Wallace's ideas.

"I would far rather burn my whole book than that he [Wallace] or any other man should think I had behaved in a paltry spirit," Darwin wrote.

But Lyell and others who knew how long Darwin had been working on his ideas presented both Darwin's and Wallace's papers at a scientific meeting on July 1, 1858. They read Darwin's first, so he received credit for thinking of the idea first. When Wallace learned that Darwin had been working on his ideas for fourteen years, he stepped aside. He let Darwin have the credit because Darwin had worked out the idea much more thoroughly than he had.

So, Darwin got busy and completed his book. It was published November 24, 1859. He was the first person to publish these views. And he was the sole target of the fury they aroused.

The Storm Breaks

"The first edition's 1,250 copies sold out the first day," says Ruth Moore in Life Nature Library's *Evolution,* "and the storm that has never wholly abated quickly broke. The indignant *Quarterly Review* charged that the book and its theory 'contradict the revealed relation of the creation to the Creator.' Another publication accused Darwin of using 'absurd facts to prop up his utterly rotten fabric of guess and speculation.'"

Darwin had not wanted to add to the prejudices against his views by discussing the origin of humans in his book. Yet he did not want "to deceive any honourable man" by concealing his views. He closed his book with one sentence: "Much light will be thrown on the origin of man and his history."

That sentence did not escape unnoticed. Darwin was damned for describing "the belief that man descends from the monkeys." At a meeting of the British Association for the Advancement of Science at Oxford University in June 1860, Bishop Samuel Wilberforce threatened to "smash Darwin." A crowd filled the meeting room. Darwin stayed away. After Wilberforce sneeringly denounced Darwin, Darwin's friend and fellow scientist Thomas H. Huxley, felt the "wildcat" in him thoroughly roused. According to Moore, "He told the audience that he would feel no shame at having an ape for an

28

This 1871 cartoon mocks Darwin's theory that man is related to animals. In the caption, the defrauded gorilla laments, "That man wants to claim my pedigree. He says he is one of my descendants."

ancestor—but that he would indeed be ashamed of a brilliant man who plunged into scientific questions of which he knew nothing. In other words, Huxley would prefer an ape to the bishop for an ancestor, and the crowd had no doubt of his meaning."

Pandemonium broke out. Men jumped to their feet shouting. One woman fainted. The former captain of the *Beagle*, Robert Fitzroy, waved a Bible and shouted "that it, rather than the viper he had harbored on his ship, was the true and unimpeachable authority," says Moore. "'Looks of bitter hatred were directed to those who were on Darwin's side,' reported *Macmillan Magazine*. Whether gentle Charles Darwin liked it or not, and he did not, the issue was fully joined—science versus religion."

Around the world, Darwin was attacked by clergy and teachers. People Darwin respected laughed at him. Sir John Herschel, a well-known British astronomer, called Darwin's theory of evolution, "the law of higgledy-piggledy." The criticism that probably hurt Darwin the worst was from his old friend, Adam Sedgwick. He had praised Darwin's work on the *Beagle* and the fossils he had sent back to England. But he wrote Darwin, "I laughed until my sides were almost sore" after reading some passages of Darwin's book. Other parts, he said, he "read with absolute sorrow, because I think them utterly false and grievously mischievous." Leading scientists of many nations were outraged by the bold new ideas in the book. The furor went on for years.

The World Would Never Be the Same

Humanity's view of the world, of life, and of itself would never be quite the same again. However people felt about Darwin's theory, it changed their thinking. The theory of evolution took science away from the spiritual world into the material, or physical, world. The Bible was no longer considered "proof" of how life came into being. The proof of evolution now would come from things that can be seen, such as fossils.

As outraged as most scientists were with Darwin's ideas, a few agreed. Huxley said that when he read Darwin's book he asked himself, "Why didn't I think of that?" Another said, "I am prepared to go to the stake for evolution."

But, is the theory of evolution true?

Most scientists believe it is. One of the reasons

Darwin's idea is so respected, Carl Sagan says, is because Darwin had gathered a "mountain of evidence." In trying to piece his evolutionary picture together, Darwin used everything known at the time in every area of biology. He collected so much evidence from all different aspects of biological and geological investigation that he demonstrated to the satisfaction of the majority of today's scientists that evolution had happened.

The Mystery of Evolution

In the more than 130 years since Darwin's ideas were first published, much evidence of evolution has been discovered. Instead of answering all the questions scientists have about evolution, though, the evidence has raised more questions. Evolution is still a mystery. But the mystery of evolution concerns its mechanism. How evolution happened is the puzzle scientists are trying to solve.

Gordon Rattray Taylor in his book, *The Great Evolution Mystery*, says, "Darwin's theory of evolution by natural selection . . . is crumbling under attack. Biologists are discovering more and more features which it does not seem able to explain."

Two scientists, Stephen Jay Gould and Niles Eldredge, propose that small changes, or *micro-evolution*, did not occur gradually, as Darwin's idea of natural selection says. Rather, they say, *punctuated equilibria* is the mechanism of evolution. Species remained the same (in equilibrium) for long periods of time, and evolution was punctuated with sudden, major changes. *Macro-evolution,* the body changes that result in origin of a new species, is the focus of study for many scientists. They are trying to find evidence to show such things as whether fins really became legs and scales became feathers and, if so, how.

Some people, even a few scientists, still believe as most people did in Darwin's day—that the world and its inhabitants were created suddenly, in a specific way and time period, by God. They believe literally the Biblical account of creation. Called Creationists, they are examining and questioning the scientific evidence that has been gathered. They are seeking evidence that they are right.

A few scientists wonder if the mechanism evolution is what one scientist calls "the hand of God." In other words, they wonder if the world and its creatures' origins might be the result of a combination of creation and evolution.

To try to solve the mystery of how evolution occurred, let us look at some of the pieces of the puzzle.

Two

What Is the Evidence?

Why do we try to solve the mystery of how evolution occurred?

Perhaps Johannes Kepler has the answer. Kepler lived a life of poverty and religious persecution. He pursued scientific studies in the 1600s, a time when people still believed in demons and witches. Kepler said, "We do not ask for what useful purpose the birds . . . sing, for song is their pleasure since they were created for singing. Similarly, we ought not to ask why the human mind troubles to fathom the secrets of the heavens. . . . The diversity of . . . Nature is so great, and the treasures hidden in the heavens so rich, precisely in order that the human mind shall never be lacking in fresh nourishment." Kepler thought that trying to unravel mysteries was food for the human mind.

So people chew on the puzzle of what "really happened." They try to solve the mystery of how evolution came about. Many of the pieces to this puzzle are found in the fossil record.

History Is Written in the Rocks

For geologists, rocks of the earth tell its history. Deposits of coal tell them that giant ferns fell into swamps between 300 and 350 million years ago,

(Opposite page) The Grand Canyon in Arizona is an important geological site. By studying the horizontal rock strata, geologists can learn about the history of the earth.

The German astronomer Johannes Kepler studied the solar system in the 1600s. Contrary to popular opinion of his day, Kepler thought it important to study the mysteries of the universe.

then slowly decayed and hardened to become coal. Banded iron formations tell them that free oxygen in the atmosphere combined with iron ions in the oceans and formed iron from 2,600 to 1,800 million years ago. Each layer of sediment, sandstone, limestone, basalt, and granite has its stories to tell.

Part of the history they relate comes from the fossils these layers contain.

An animal or plant can only become a fossil if it is buried quickly and if some part of it is tough enough to be preserved. After it is buried, water seeps into the bone, shell, or other hard part and is absorbed. The bone or shell calcifies, or becomes like calcium.

Sometimes minerals replace bones, shells, and other hard parts as they are dissolved. Sometimes brightly colored silica calcite or orange and red iron components become a part of the fossil bone or shell.

A fossil may be a mold of the original organism. Sometimes the original shell or skeletal material may be dissolved and not replaced. Then it leaves a mold of the fossil in the surrounding rock. Plants may also leave imprints.

For scientists, reading the fossil record is like reading a book. They read the story of the evolution of life.

The Fossil Story

The oldest fossils that have been found are between three and three-and-a-half billion years old. Some of these microscopic fossils have been identified as blue-green algae and bacteria because they resemble blue-green algae and bacteria of today. These organisms were a very simple form of life. They were one-celled, but that cell was not even as complicated as a human cell, which scientists call *eucaryote* (pronounced *you carry oat*) or "true nucleus."

We do not think of cells as being complicated, perhaps because it takes billions of cells to make up our bodies. But a cell is like a miniature factory. It is full of "workers" that combine food with oxygen to extract energy. The cell nucleus is like a "boss" in the cell factory. These first life forms that scientists call *procaryotes* cells had no nucleus. They were sort of pre-cell creatures.

Some time later in the fossil record, one-celled organisms appear, then multi-celled organisms. More and more complicated organisms show up in the fossil record. These more complicated life forms mark the beginning of sexual reproduction, scientists believe.

Microscopic organisms that appear in a single drop of water. Did all life evolve from simple organisms such as these?

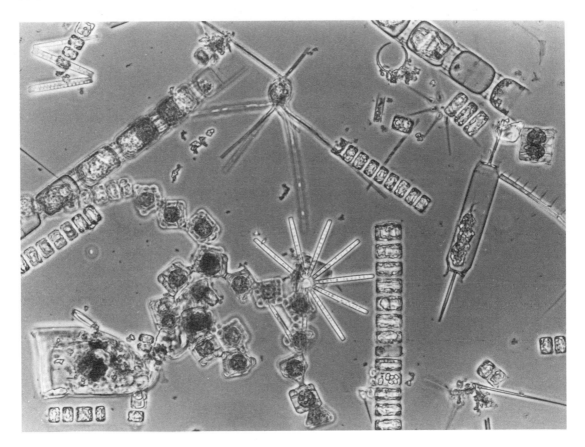

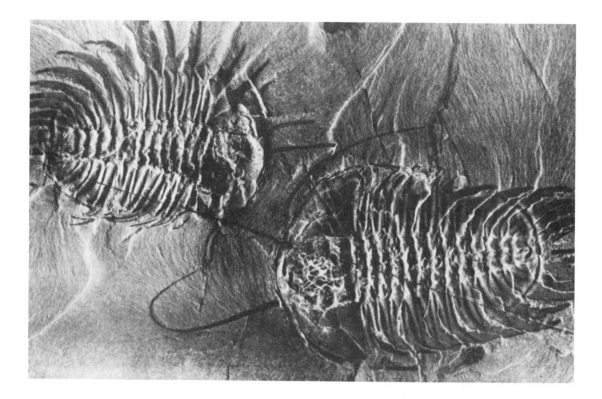

Numerous trilobite fossils lead scientists to believe that this animal lived abundantly during the Cambrian period. The trilobite is now extinct.

Initially, organisms increased their population by simply splitting in two. It was like an offspring having one parent. There was little chance for change. Sexual reproduction allowed offspring to draw genes from two parents. There was more opportunity for a "mixing up" of genes.

Then suddenly, at the beginning of what scientists call the Cambrian period, about 570 million years ago, life exploded. ("Suddenly" in evolutionist's eyes can mean fifty million years.) Scientists believe this was when free oxygen entered the picture. Breathing is more efficient than drawing energy from the fermentation process that earlier microscopic life used. At first, oxygen was a pollutant. Many organisms died. No further trace of them is found in the fossil record. Others retreated to the bottom of the sea. One animal that succeeded well in this new environment, judging by the number of fossils found, is the trilobite, now extinct.

All these early forms of life lived in the sea. Some of them were jellyfish, plankton, corals, snails, sponges, and starfish. They were invertebrates; they had no backbone.

Then, fossils show, around 500 million years ago, some of these marine creatures had *notochords,* which are solid, gristle-like backbones. Notochords evolved into vertebrates, or segmented backbones. Then "bony" fish make their appearance in the fossil record. Fish were the first animals to have an inside skeleton. (Some creatures, like the starfish, have external skeletons.) The bony fish were of two kinds. One was ray-finned fish, which are like the fish we catch when fishing today. The other were lobe-finned fish, which took evolution on a different path, onto land.

Before lobe-finned fish could make that move

A rendition of Cambrian submarine landscape. Many early forms of life lived in the sea.

Scientists believe that the lung fish evolved because of a lack of oxygen in the seas. The fish learned to rise from the sea and breathe in the oxygen necessary for survival.

"The millions of species of animals and plants that have ever lived on the Earth all evolved from a single ancestry by a natural process over hundreds of millions of years. Such change is beautifully revealed in the fossil record of past life."

Science writer Roy Gallant, *Fossils*

"The vast fossil record, comprising as it does, a worldwide cemetery preserved in stone for men everywhere to see, is not at all a record of the gradual evolution of life, but rather of the sudden destruction of lives."

Creation Scientist Dr. Henry M. Morris, *Remarkable Birth*

to land, though, they had to make a change. They had to be able to breathe out of water. By this time, oxygen had increased greatly, both in the ocean and in the atmosphere.

A Fish Story

From the fossil record, scientists piece together the story of what might have happened when lung fish came into being. At that time, the ocean had receded. Perhaps the small basins of water got "old" or "stuffy," as one scientist calls it. There was not enough oxygen in the stuffy water, so fish surged out of the water to gulp in the oxygen they needed. By this time, the oxygen in the atmosphere was creating the ozone layer, which would keep off the worst of the sun's heat. Creatures were not in danger of being fried by the sun if they left the water.

As more land became dry, rain collected and formed freshwater ponds and rivers. Some of these fish, stranded perhaps by the receding ocean, or in search of less stuffy water, scooted into fresh water. Many probably died because the oceans were as salty then as they are today. And those fish needed salt water to live. But some of those early fish adapted to their environment. They learned to live in the fresh water. The ray-finned fish remained there. They are the ancestors of today's fish found in lakes and rivers.

The fossil record shows that lobe-finned lung fish took another evolutionary path, perhaps because their lobe fins required more and stronger muscles. Some developed into amphibians, animals who lived both in water and on land, like crocodiles, frogs, and salamanders. Their legs still come out from the sides of their bodies, as their lobe fins once had. Keeping themselves moist while living out of water presented a problem for amphibians. Their thick skins helped keep their bodies moist. They continued to lay their eggs in water, as most amphibians do today, to keep their jelly-like eggs from drying out.

Later, some amphibians evolved into reptiles, like the alligators. Still cold-blooded like amphib-

A crocodile from the Congo in Africa. Lizard-like crocodiles and alligators evolved from amphibians.

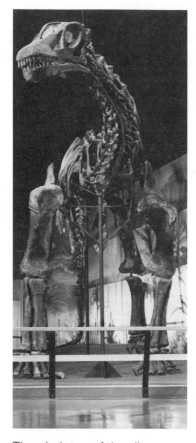

The skeleton of the dinosaur *Haplocanthosaurus delfsi* mounted at the Cleveland Museum of Natural History. The reasons for the disappearance of dinosaurs are the subject of much debate and controversy.

ians, reptiles also live both in land and water. But they do not need the water quite as much as amphibians do. Reptiles adapted even more to their environment. Their pelvic bones shifted, so legs came out from underneath their bodies. That meant they could walk more easily.

But the reptiles' big step forward in evolution was the *amniote egg*, which is something like a chicken egg. The tough-shelled egg gave embryos, the undeveloped young, their own liquid environment in which to develop. The amniotic fluid is salty like the sea.

Reptiles evolved into different branches. One branch of the reptile family were the dinosaurs. But from another branch, called the thecodonts, came the first mammals, the first warm-blooded animals. Pointy-faced and sharp-toothed little creatures that are thought to have looked a little like opossums, they lived at the same time dinosaurs dominated the earth. Because they were small, they did not threaten the existence of the dinosaurs. After the dinosaurs became extinct, mammals evolved into many species as different as pigs and whales, including—after millions of years—humans.

The Human Family

There are enough fossils of many animals so that scientists can trace their evolution. From fossils found in the United States, scientists trace how a mustang or thoroughbred horse developed from a cat-sized animal with three toes into a large, long-legged animal with hooves. They can also tell that horses became extinct in America during one of the ice ages. If these animals had not crossed the Bering bridge into Asia before the worst of the cold hit, there would have been no horses for the Spaniards to bring into this country again in the 1500s.

But the fossil record for humans has many missing pieces. Human bones are much more fragile than animal bones. So most of what scientists know about human evolution is based on conjecture rather than fossils. Conjecture is something like an educated guess. It is like looking at the hole left in a jigsaw puzzle by a missing piece and deciding from the shape of the hole what shape the missing piece is. During the history of science, these conjectures have been proved right many times. But sometimes they have been wrong. That puzzle hole, for instance, might not be for a single missing piece, it might contain two or three smaller pieces that show something altogether different.

The fossil of Neanderthal man was found shortly before Darwin published his book. A skull and some limb bones were found in a cave in the Neander Valley, Germany. Named for where he was found (*thal* means *valley* in German), Neanderthal man caused some disagreement among scientists.

An artistic rendition of Neanderthal man. Many scientists believe that Neanderthal man, who flourished 200,000 years ago, is in modern man's direct line of descent.

A diorama depicts *Homo erectus,* or erect-walking man. These early men made stone tools, used fire, and developed a language.

Today, with modern testing skills, scientists have determined that Neanderthal man was two hundred thousand years old. But when the bones were first discovered, many scientists still did not believe the world was more than six thousand years old. So some scientists thought the bones no more than fifty years old. Some thought they belonged to a Russian Cossack who had run away from Napoleon's army fifty years earlier and hid in a cave to escape detection. Others thought they might be the bones of a Celt.

Most people who saw those fossil bones thought they belonged to a "brutish" man, not somebody like themselves. They did not want to believe this creature with its heavy eyebrow ridges and abnormally thick skull could be an *ancestor* of humans. No one took Neanderthal man seriously as a fossil. His bones were stuck in a closet. It would be some years before scientists decided that this small-brained man with the heavy-ridged, sloping forehead was a human ancestor. But scientists are still arguing about just where he fits in the human evolutionary picture.

Although scientists in the 1800s rejected Neanderthal man as a human ancestor, some students of the past kept digging for other human fossils. In a cave in the Cro-Magnon area in southern France, they found many fossils. Cro-Magnon man was found. Some skeletons were so complete they were almost indistinguishable from skeletons of modern humans. Even the most stubborn scientists had to admit they were human fossils. Then people began to argue about how old the fossils were. Many scientists still refused to believe the world was older than six thousand years.

Many fossils have been found in the more than one hundred years since those *hominid* (human or near-human) bones were first discovered in the Neander Valley. At first, fossils were named for the lo-

"The only Bible-honoring conclusion is . . . that Genesis I-II is the actual historical truth, regardless of any scientific or chronologic problems thereby entailed."

Creation Scientist Dr. Henry Morris, *Scientific Creationism*

"Why does our body, from the bones of our back to the muscles of our belly, display vestiges of an arrangement better suited for quadrupedal life if we aren't descendants of four-footed creatures?"

Dr. Stephen Jay Gould, *Discover* Magazine, January 1987

A bust of Cro-Magnon man, named after the site in France where his remains were discovered. Most experts agree that Cro-Magnon man closely resembles modern man.

A fossil of australopithecine man. Many scientists believe that the related species *Australopithecus afarensis* is the first certain ancestor of man.

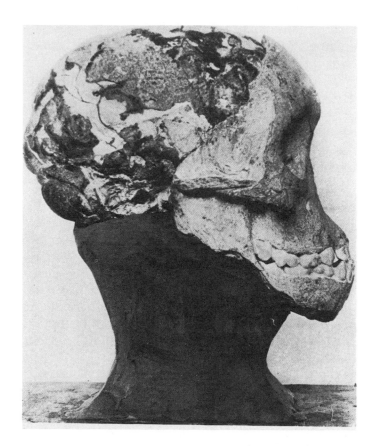

cation in which they were found: Java man, Peking man, Heidelberg man, and Cro-Magnon. Later, scientists chose species names that would describe them: *Homo habilis* (handy man), *Homo erectus* (erect man), *Homo sapiens* (wise or thinking man).

Java Man

Fossil hunters did not have an easy time of it. When fossil hunter and physician Eugène Dubois was looking for Java man, he was competing with people who were searching for "dragon bones" for the Chinese. Ground "dragon bones" brought a high price as medicines.

Dubois' Java man fossil, found in the 1890s, caused confusion, too. Dubois was certain he had found a human-like ape, the "missing link" between apes and humans that many people were looking for. Scientists disagreed with him. They thought Java man was a human. Dubois was angered by the rejection of his ideas. He carried *Pithecanthropus erectus* (ape-man walking erect) home and buried him beneath his dining room floor. He refused to let any scientists see or speak about the fossil. Later, when other fossils were found, the scientists were proved right. Java man was human. Today, Java man carries the species name *Homo erectus*, erect-walking man. He, and others with his name, are humans, but they were different from modern humans.

In 1924, fossils turned up in Africa in a limestone quarry. It was later found that other fossils had been destroyed in several limestone quarries before somebody recognized their importance. No one had expected to find human fossils in Africa. Those fossils were named *Australopithecus africanus*—the southern (Australo) ape (pithecus) from Africa. The australopithecines would go on to make history.

What Do Fossils Mean?

A human fossil may be no more than a jaw bone, a skull, or even only part of a skull. Scientists can tell a great deal about what sort of creature has been found and when it lived by examining just a single molar. An australopithecine, for instance, has very big back teeth, much larger than human teeth, and the enamel is much thicker.

In order to learn what tooth belongs to what sort of animal, scientists must keep careful records. "The only way a scientist can start to understand anything is to describe it, to measure it, and name it," Donald Johanson says in his book *Lucy, The Beginnings of Humankind*. Johanson is a paleoanthropologist, one who studies human fossils. He

"Since Darwin's time, of course, fossilized bones of hundreds of creatures intermediate between apes and modern humans have been discovered. It is no longer possible for a reasonable person to deny that what once seemed absurd [human evolution] actually happened."

Jared Diamond, *Discover* Magazine

"Although the fossil record has been interpreted to teach evolution, the record itself has been based on the assumption of evolution. . . . The fossils speak of evolution, because they have been *made* to speak of evolution."

Creation scientist Dr. Henry M. Morris, *Scientific Creationism* says if he studied the skulls of ten people, he would find wide differences in brain size and facial measurements.

And, if a half a million years from now, somebody were to dig up those same ten skulls, and if they came from different parts of the world, and if some of them were so crushed that one could not really measure them properly, and if some had their teeth missing, and if some others were represented only by a few teeth, and if—on top of that—there could be no certainty that all of them really were a half a million years old, what could he do?

He would concentrate on the differences, and

A nineteenth-century excavating site photo captures archaeologists searching for the remains of prehistoric man in France.

measure everything carefully. He would study this one and compare it with that one, and what would impress him would be those differences. It took a long time for anthropologists to get it through their own skulls that populations are extremely variable. Therefore one has to have a big sample—men, women and children—before one can begin to recognize the features that are common to them all. With such a sample, one begins to get not only a sense of the consistent features of the population but also a sense of its variability.

First Family

A fossil nicknamed Lucy is a member of what many scientists call the First Family. Her fossil and those of thirteen people who lived at the same time she did were found in the Afar desert in Ethiopia in 1974 and 1975. She died three-and-a-half million years ago.

The temperature was 110 degrees Fahrenheit in the Ethiopian desert on November 30, 1974, the day Donald Johanson found Lucy. The rocks gave off heat like stoves, but Johanson had decided it was a lucky day. He went first with a coworker to survey one of the sites being excavated in the Afar desert. After surveying for a couple of hours, his coworker was ready to head back to camp. But Johanson said, "Let's go back this way and survey the bottom of that little gully over there." The gully had been thoroughly checked out at least twice before and nothing interesting had been found. But that "lucky" feeling had been with Johanson since he woke, so he decided to make that small final detour. Luck plays a part in fossil-finding, Johanson says. They are extremely rare. Many scientists look for fossils all their lives and never find one.

"There was virtually no bone in the gully," Johanson says. "But as we turned to leave, I noticed

"The development of speech was the most important reason for the increase in the size of the human brain."

Zoologist Ernst Mayr, *Omni Interviews*

"Brain growth was stimulated by increased meat-eating . . . because you can't eat sufficient amounts of meat to survive unless you've got sharp implements to cut with. . . . Increased technology stimulated the evolution of the brain."

Paleontologist Richard Leakey, *Omni Interviews*

something lying on the ground part way up the slope." And there he discovered the first bones of the fossil that would make history. Sometime during the party's celebration that night, a tape played over and over. It was the Beatles' recording of "Lucy in the Sky with Diamonds." And Lucy got her name.

Lucy is unusual because so many of her bones have been found. That tells scientists that she died quietly, says Johanson. "There were no tooth marks on her bones. They had not been crunched or splintered, as they would have been if she had been killed by a lion or a saber-toothed cat."

There are not many old skeletons. Usually only fragments are found—a tooth here, part of a jaw bone there, or a leg bone, maybe a complete skull. Lucy's bones, though, number more than two dozen, from pieces of skull to lower leg bones. From those bones, scientists can tell that Lucy was about three and one-half feet tall and that she weighed about sixty pounds. But she was an adult, probably twenty-five to thirty years old, according to Johanson. Her head, judging by the skull fragments recovered, was only a little larger than a softball.

Seen from a distance, Lucy might be mistaken for a human. She walked upright and possibly even ran on two legs, which apes cannot do. Seen up close, though, she would not be mistaken for a human. Her head would have looked like a gorilla's head. She had no chin. She had bony ridges over her eyes. Her forehead was not smoothly rounded as ours are today. There would not have been room enough in her head for a modern human brain.

Australopithecines

Lucy's scientific name is *Australopithecus afarensis*. The last part of her name tells where she was found, in the Afar desert. But Lucy is also ho-

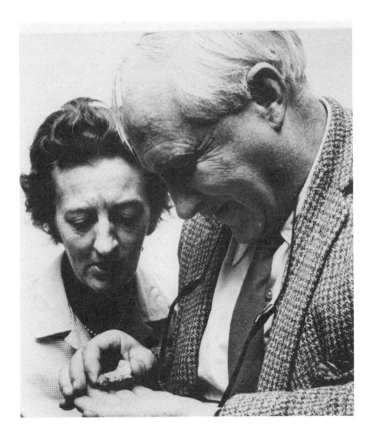

Paleontologist Louis Leakey and his wife Mary display a recent fossil find. In 1962, Leakey discovered *Homo habilis*, or "handy man." Fossils indicate that these people used simple tools to hunt and prepare wild animals for food.

minid, which is what scientists call an erect-walking primate. She is either an extinct ancestor to humans, a human relative, or a true human. There was no abrupt crossover from ape to human, Johanson explains. Human evolution was gradual. Over time, primates began to be less and less ape-like and more human-like. That group of humans and near-humans is hominid.

Lucy and her kind have cousins: *Australopithecus africanus* and *Australopithecus robustus*. *A. africanus* is a small, fragile creature like Lucy's family but did not live quite as long ago. At least no fossils dating back that far have been found. *A. robustus*, as the name implies, would probably have made good football linebackers. They were husky folks. They are the most recent of all the australopithecines.

Lucy and her cousins walked as we do. Forty-seven footprints discovered by paleontologist Mary Leakey frozen in lava prove that. They look much like our footprints.

These hominids had other human features. Their hands were more human than ape. Their thumbs were *opposable*, which means the hominids could pinch things between thumb and forefinger. They had small molar teeth like ours. But in some ways they were unlike humans. Their brains were much smaller, between 430 to 550 cubic centimeters (cc). Human brains measure from 1,000 to 1,800 cc. Also, Lucy and her cousins left behind no tools, and humans use tools.

Australopithecines have been found in sixteen different places in South Africa, East Africa, and

A jawbone of a primitive being (right) is contrasted with that of a modern man (left). The massive teeth of the primitive jawbone show harsh wear, suggesting a gritty diet.

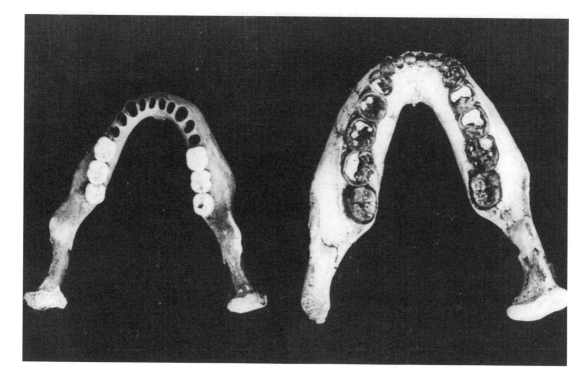

An artist's version of a
Neanderthal family preparing
a fire.

Ethiopia, which is in northeast Africa.

Next in the picture of human evolution, according to the fossil record, comes *Homo habilis*, "handy" man, whose brains were slightly larger than australopithecines (500-800 cc). The first fossils of this oldest known human were found first and identified by Louis Leakey, paleontologist husband of Mary Leakey, in East Africa in 1962. Louis Leakey was a colorful scientist who at times made claims for his finds that did not hold up. His first fossil of *H. habilis* was not readily accepted by other scientists. But Leakey, raised in Kenya, had collected ancient tools as a child. He knew he would one day find his tool maker.

A second fossil, located later, proved him right. It was Louis who later named these people *Homo habilis.* They were makers of simple tools. A hand-sized stone had flakes chipped off of one side to make a sharp edge. Scientists believe that a million years ago all people used such tools to cut animal carcasses into manageable pieces. Some people use such tools even today.

H. habilis fossils have been found only along East Africa's Great Rift Valley. The fossil record shows that *Homo habilis* lived for about five hundred thousand years. They gathered wild foods, hunted small game, and scavenged occasionally from dead elephants and rhinos. Then *Homo habilis* disappeared and *Homo erectus* came on the scene.

Homo Erectus

The first fossil found and identified as *Homo erectus* was of a twelve-year-old boy. He, like Lucy, died a quiet death. Scientists know this because almost all of his skeleton was found where it had apparently washed into a marsh one and a half million years ago in what is now Kenya, East Africa. Although those teeth sometimes called twelve-year molars had not completely grown in, he was already five feet, six inches tall. Had he lived, he might have become six feet tall. The largest *Homo erectus* brain found is 1,250 cc, larger than a small modern brain. *Homo erectus* lived in communities. They lived in homes built of stone or wood where they used tools not only for chopping meat but for scraping hides and cutting skins into clothes.

During the million years they lived, *Homo erectus* walked out of Africa and into Asia and Europe. Fossils found in a cave in Beijing, China, show they lived there for 200,000 years. Their brains grew 70 cc during that time. Ashes and charcoal show they used fires. Scientists believe they stole fire "from the wild," where lightning might have started it. *Homo erectus* had to keep their fire going, so flints and rubbing sticks came along farther on the evolutionary trail.

Homo erectus were skilled hunters, trapping or slaughtering large game like deer and elephants. They lived when gigantic mammals roamed the earth.

Homo erectus had large teeth, so the jaw jutted out, but they had no chin. Some skulls found in Europe had smaller faces with smaller teeth, a low forehead, and small chin. Those fossils called Java man, Peking man, and Heidelberg man have been identified as *Homo erectus*. *Homo erectus* became extinct two hundred thousand years ago.

Homo Sapiens

The next rung up on the evolutionary ladder is *Homo sapiens*, thinking, or wise, man. *Homo sapiens's* skulls were larger to accommodate larger brains which, like our brains today, measured from 1,000 to 2,000 cubic centimeters.

The oldest of these fossils belong to the same family as Neanderthal man. They had distinct foreheads, which were low. Their eyebrow ridge was heavy, but their teeth were small and they had a

Reconstruction of head and skull of a Peking woman, named after the location in which she was found.

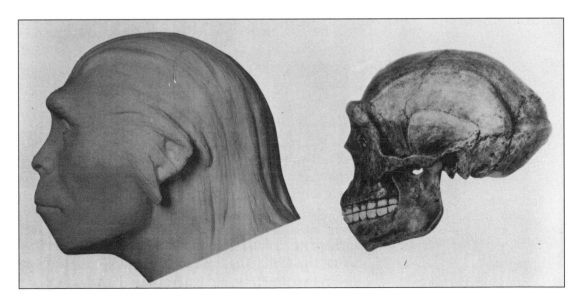

small chin. For the first time in the fossil record, though, burial grounds were found among the homes and workplaces that have been found all over Europe, in the Middle East, and in Asia. They buried their people in cemeteries, and they buried them with flowers. They were beginning to think about themselves in new ways. So scientists call these people *Homo sapiens*, but add the subspecies name of *neanderthalis*, to indicate that they are different from modern people. The oldest fossils are probably 300 thousand years old, which means they lived at the same time as did *Homo erectus,* from whom they descended. But after *H. erectus* became extinct, *neanderthalis* lived on for 250 thousand years.

Homo sapiens neanderthalis were replaced by *Homo sapiens sapiens*, the subspecies that includes all humans living today. For ten thousand years, *H. sapiens neanderthalis* and *H. sapiens sapiens* lived at the same time. *H. sapiens sapiens* appear in the fossil record fifty thousand years ago. Their foreheads were larger and smoothly rounded, with brow ridges much less apparent. Their chins were much more distinct. Modern human teeth are smaller and require less jawbone to hold them. The fossil record shows that as *H. sapiens sapiens* moved westward out of Asia and across Europe, *neanderthalis* disappeared.

What Happened to *Neanderthalis*?

Why did *neanderthalis* disappear as modern humans moved into their territory? This is one of the unsolved mysteries of evolution. No fossil evidence has been found to give a reasonably certain answer. However, some scientists theorize that modern humans may have hunted *neanderthalis* to extinction. Others believe *neanderthalis* may have been absorbed into the modern human population through intermarriage. Some scientists believe *nean-*

derthalis had thick, compact bodies because they lived in a glacial period and they died out because they could not survive the warming that occurred.

Most scientists today believe the fossil record supports Darwin's idea of evolution and natural selection and that organisms made many small and gradual changes as they adapted to their environment.

Different Views

Other scientists disagree. They think the fossil record shows that there were "jumps" in evolution that Darwin's idea does not explain.

Still other scientists think the fossil record shows that natural selection is only part of the story of how evolution occurs. Natural selection, they say, may have brought about the small changes, or *micro-evolution*. But the major changes, *macro-evolution*, that bring about new species came in "jumps."

Another group of people, called Creationists, believe that both those groups of scientists are reading the fossil record incorrectly. They have their own interpretation.

Who is right? What is their evidence? Is the fossil record the only evidence of evolution?

Three

Do All Scientists Agree with Darwin?

How did evolution happen? How, for instance, did that first small sharp-faced mammal with pointy teeth evolve into such species as the whale and humans?

Darwin's theory says it occurred by natural selection. Small changes occurred by chance gradually over millions of years. The changes came about as plants and animals, organisms, adapted to their environment. Eventually, all those small changes brought about new species.

Carl Sagan agrees. "Humans have deliberately selected which plants and animals shall live and which shall die for thousands of years," Carl Sagan says. "Ten thousand years ago, there were no dairy cows or ferret hounds or large ears of corn. When we domesticated the ancestors of these plants and animals . . . we controlled their breeding."

The process is called *artificial selection* because humans, not nature, choose which animals or plants to breed. "The enormous distended udders of dairy cattle are the result of a human interest in milk and cheese. Our corn, or maize, has been bred for ten thousand generations to be more tasty and nutritious than its scrawny ancestors," writes Sagan.

If humans can cause such genetic changes by

(Opposite page) A lemur from Madagascar peers from a tree. In the nineteenth century, Charles Darwin was denounced for suggesting that humans may share a common ancestor with animals such as this.

Carl Sagan believes that chance accounts for much of the evolutionary process. Random chance, Sagan maintains, determines which traits are passed from generation to generation.

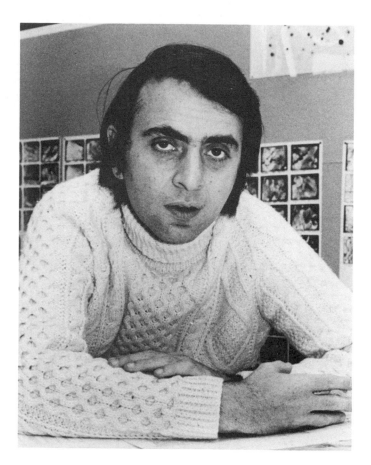

crossbreeding in ten thousand years, Sagan asks, what can nature do over millions of years? "The essence of artificial selection," he says, "is this: Many physical and behavioral traits of plants and animals are inherited. They breed true."

Random Chance

In natural selection, according to Darwin's theory, random chance determines which traits are passed on. Sagan sees chance at work in evolution, as Darwin did. He says, "Were the Earth to be started over again with all its physical features identical, it is extremely unlikely that anything closely resembling a human being would ever again emerge. There is a powerful random character to the evolutionary process. . . . Perhaps if one less dragonfly had drowned in the Carboniferous swamps, the intelligent organisms on our planet today would have feathers and teach their young in rookeries. . . . The incompleteness of our understanding humbles us."

An example of random chance in natural selection at work was recorded by scientists in England.

The Evolution of Moths

In the mid-1800s, peppered moths were light colored with tiny dark patches, the same color as the tree lichens they lighted on. Their camouflage protected them from the birds that wanted to eat them. Occasionally, a dark-colored peppered moth was born. Because birds could see the dark moths, they were probably eaten before they could reproduce.

Then the industrial revolution occurred in England. Its pollution killed the tree lichens and blackened the tree bark. Now light-colored moths stood out, easily spotted by birds that wanted to eat them. Within fifty years, white moths became rare. The majority of moths were dark-colored. Evolution was seen at work.

But the evolution of these moths was not over. When England passed its clean-air act and industries cleaned up their pollution, lichen came back to the trees. The trees themselves lost their blackened bark. Now the dark moths were again easy prey for birds. They were eaten before they could have young. Evolution was at work again. Those rare white moths that had survived were now favored. They lived to produce young. Within fifty years, most of the peppered moths were light colored again.

As fascinated as scientists are that this example of evolution at work happened in a short enough

"We are surrounded from babyhood by familiar farm and domestic animals, fruits and trees and vegetables. Where do they come from? Were they once free-living in the wild? . . . No . . . they are, most of them, made by us [by means of] artificial-selection. . . . But, if humans can make new varieties of plants and animals, must not nature do so also? This related process is called natural selection . . . the great discovery associated with the names of Charles Darwin and Alfred Russel Wallace."

Dr. Carl Sagan, *Cosmos*

"Darwin's theory of evolution by natural selection . . . is crumbling under attack. Biologists are discovering more and more features which it does not seem able to explain."

British Television science advisor Gordon Rattray Taylor, *The Great Evolution Mystery*

Why isn't the ostrich able to fly? According to Darwin's theory, animals evolve to survive a particular environment. Yet the inability to fly does not seem to be an advantageous trait.

time to be observed, they do not agree on what it means.

To some, perhaps most, it is evidence that evolution occurs as Darwin thought: Species that adapt to their environment survive and pass on to their offspring the characteristic that helped them survive. With the moths, that characteristic was color.

For other scientists, it raised a question: Why did not all the light-colored moths become extinct?

Still others agree that it is an example of natural selection as Darwin saw it, but it does not explain how small changes accumulate until they bring about macro-evolution, the major changes that create a new species. It does not explain, for example, how a certain group of dinosaurs became birds.

Darwin's Theory Explains Too Much

Darwin's theory "explains" too much, says Gordon Rattray Taylor in his book *The Great Evolution Mystery.* "If a creature acquires a new feature, it can always be argued that it was advantageous," he says.

But why, he asks, is warm-bloodedness an advantage to some fish, but not others? If flight is an advantage to birds, why are there birds like the emu, kiwi, and ostrich that do not fly? Why did the Irish elk develop antlers that were twelve feet across, weighing about two hundred and fifty pounds when their size made life so difficult? Why did some early organisms continue to evolve or become extinct while the oyster has lived on relatively unchanged?

Some organisms evolve when there does not seem to be any cause. Others, says Taylor, do not fit well in their environment and, according to Darwin's thinking, should evolve by adapting to their environment, but do not.

The Amniotic Egg

Darwin argues that evolutionary change always moves forward, says Taylor. But does it? he asks, as he looks at the evolutionary change of reptiles laying eggs on land.

The amniotic egg is a miracle, he says. The egg shell is rigid enough to protect its cargo but not so rigid that baby creatures cannot peck their way out. It also allows the chick to breathe. The yolk is sus-

A series of photographs records an ostrich hatching from its shell. Darwin believed that the amniotic egg was the result of gradual evolution.

pended in the middle of the egg, supported by threads. You can rotate the shell of an egg twenty times without disturbing the yolk. The threads just wind up. The egg white, or albumen, is remarkable.

The reptile egg, though somewhat different than today's bird egg, Taylor says, is a "stunning advance" from a "blob of jelly that constitutes eggs of fish and frogs. No longer did the land-living vertebrates have to return to the sea or river to lay their eggs," says Taylor, "for their eggs had their own private pools of liquid to float in. So [the animals] could wander freely over the earth." It allowed them to diversify.

But if all evolutionary change is for the better, as Darwin purports, why, then, Taylor asks, did some animals return to the sea. Why did one of the dinosaurs, the ichthyosaur, go back to living in the water?

"The argument that the reptiles succeeded so well because the amniote egg opened new possibilities of finding a living begins to look extremely shaky. What was the point of having this wonderful new gimmick, if you were going to compete with the well-established fish anyway?"

Evolution Does Not Explain Major Change

The egg is a stunning creation, Taylor says, but it is not the result of gradual evolution as Darwin theorizes. It is a *saltation*, or a "jump" in evolution. The fossil record does not show how this happened.

The fossil record does not show many of the changes that occur in *speciation*, development of a new species, he says.

In the transition to land, he points out, fish needed to make many changes. They needed:

• Legs to relieve the pressure of the body on the ground, which would have compressed the lungs.

• A strong pelvic girdle to support the legs.

• A stronger spine.

A dozen dinosaur eggs. Why did some animals go back to the sea when the amniotic egg allowed them to bear offspring on land?

• Stronger bone. Without strong bones, he says, terrestrial, or land, creatures could not support themselves against the drag of gravity. Creation of bone alone required a "whole burst" of mutations.

• Protection from drying out. Eyes needed tears to stay moist and eyelids as protection from dust. The nose needed mucus protection.

• Changed sense organs. Ears were needed both to detect sound and to preserve balance by analyzing how the body is moving. Eyes had to change because air refracts light differently than water.

The change from reptile to bird means a lot of change beside scales to feathers, Taylor says.

• The body had to be condensed into a compact shape.

• The pelvis had to be strengthened to absorb the shock of landing.

• Legs and feet had to be reduced to a minimum; the vanished leg muscles had to be replaced by muscles within the body.

• The brain had to be modified to handle problems of balance and coordination.

• Larger vision became more important than smell.

• Body metabolism needed a lot of fuel to maintain high temperature.

• Partitions of the heart had to be completed.

• Lungs had to be enlarged and supplemented by air spaces in the body.

The fossil record, says Taylor, lacks the intermediate stages that these creatures went through.

The Missing Links

"Missing links" have always intrigued people. Some scientists, like Eugène Dubois, became fossil hunters solely in order to look for those missing links, the "bridges" between one species and another.

Some transition organisms have been found.

"Neanderthals are held by most scientists to have been a side branch on the evolutionary tree, a branch that died out."

Science writer Gene Bylinsky, *Life in Darwin's Universe*

". . . [According to] Milford H. Wolpoff, University of Michigan . . . Neanderthals . . . evolved into today's Europeans."

Science writer Boyce Rensberger in *Mosaic Reader: Human Evolution*

An illustration of *archaeopteryx*, the primitive bird that retained reptilian skeletal features. The discovery of the *archaeopteryx* fossil supports Darwin's theory that change occurred slowly over time.

"Some [scientists] . . . have suggested . . . that invading moderns interbred with the Neanderthals and absorbed their physical characteristics. . . . It is inconceivable that Neanderthal characteristics would have been so completely masked out."

Dr. Niles Eldredge, *The Myths of Human Evolution*

"You look at . . . the distinctive features of modern Europeans . . . and then you look at the fossil populations to see where those features first appear, and . . . every feature can be found in [one or another] Neanderthal [fossil] sample."

Michigan University Professor Milford H. Wolpoff, *Mosaic Reader: Human Evolution*

One is a creature called *Seymouria* (because it was found in Seymour, Texas). It is, Taylor says, "almost exactly intermediate in structure between amphibians and reptiles."

Among the most remarkable fossils are several skeletons that were found in southern Germany. These skeletons "are clearly transitional between birds and their reptilian ancestors," says A. Lee McAlister, of Southern Methodist University, in *The History of Life*. The skeletons have teeth (all modern birds are toothless). And other features are so much like those of certain small dinosaurs that if nothing but the skeletons had been preserved, they probably would have been described as reptiles.

"Fortunately," says McAlister, "the fine-grained limestone in which the skeletons are preserved also shows clear impressions of flight feathers on the tail and on the elongated front limbs. Feathers, found only in birds, indicate that this strange animal was indeed a primitive bird that still retained the skeletal features of its reptilian ancestors." The transitional bird is *archaeopteryx*.

The fossil record shows other evidence of gradual change, according to paleontologist Thomas J.M. Schopf, from the University of Chicago. One example he gives is a marine creature called the *cephalopod*. "Over millions of years, it underwent steady changes in size and shape of its living chambers and in its ornamentation. The differences have been resolved into six species."

Just because the fossil record shows little or no change in bones or shells of a species over time does not mean the entire animal remains unchanged, he adds. Soft parts do not fossilize, he points out. The soft parts may change radically while the hard parts remain *static*.

Missing Pages in the Fossil Record

Because conditions have to be just right to make fossils, many plants and animals undoubtedly lived but left no mark of their existence. So there are holes in the fossil records. Those holes cause confu-

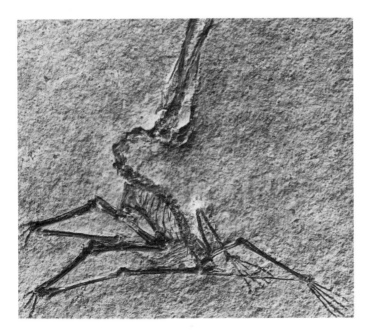

A well-preserved fossil provides clues to primitive life on earth. However, many animals did not leave such striking evidence of their existence.

Stephen Jay Gould proposed that evolution is marked with rapid changes as species adapt to their environment.

sion among scientists.

In addition, just because something shows up suddenly in the fossil record does not mean it evolved suddenly, states geneticist Russell Lande from the University of Chicago.

He says, "Fossil sites are rare, widely scattered places where conditions are right for preserving bones and where erosion has reexposed the fossils." The absence of the "missing links," when one species was evolving into another, Lande says, could well be explained if the transition took place in a small, geographically isolated region. The animal's sudden appearance in the fossil record might mean it had just migrated into the region being sampled.

Lande believes the theory of evolution does explain species change. But he wondered how animals managed in intermediate stages with such things as half-formed limbs, stumps, and half-wings. He began to research that area. When studying dugongs (close relatives of sea cows) who lived about 45 million years ago, he found that each stage of transition animal was a thriving species. The changes were so small and there were so many gradations, he said, that taxonomists (classifiers of organisms) have been at a loss as to how to classify the animals.

So Lande concludes that intermediate stages of limb development can be adaptive, or at least not severely handicap the animal. This means that a major evolutionary change such as complete limb loss need not have arisen as a single jump.

Another View

Two scientists who found such "jumps" in evolution puzzling proposed that evolution occurred somewhat differently than Darwin theorized. They are Stephen Jay Gould, professor of geology at the Museum of Comparative Zoology at Harvard University, and Niles Eldredge, curator of invertebrates at the American Museum of Natural History. Their answer to this mystery is called *punctuated equilibria* mentioned in chapter one. Remember that Gould and Eldredge believe that species remain the same (equilibrium) for long periods of time, then evolve, not gradually as Darwin thought, but rapidly. Evolution is punctuated with these rapid changes.

Punctuated equilibria does not disagree with all of Darwin's theory, Eldredge says. It agrees that small changes occur in a species during those long periods of stability, or *stasis,* as the species adapts to its environment. But a new species does not come about as a result of gradual change.

Darwin's idea also says that all individuals of a species change or evolve. Gould and Eldredge believe that speciation happens to the group when a small part of a species population is separated from the rest. Because there are fewer animals involved, there are fewer genes. So the combination and recombination (or "mixing up") of genes and muta-

The frozen, preserved carcass of a baby mammoth that lived forty thousand years ago was discovered in 1977. Why is the mammoth now extinct?

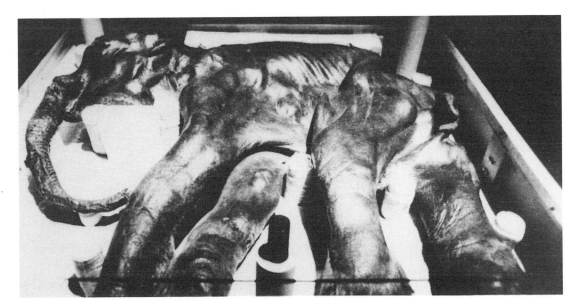

tions bring change about rapidly.

To prove their theory, Gould and Eldredge set out with a group of other scientists to trace the evolutionary life of backboneless organisms which they could collect by the thousands. The large number of fossils they could find would enable them to make a detailed study.

Eldredge chose a distinctive trilobite that lived during the middle Devonion period, between 350 and 400 million years ago, but is now extinct. One unique feature of this trilobite was that it had eighteen columns of lenses in each eye. As Eldredge uncovered more and more trilobite fossils that spanned eighteen million years, he found only one change. Some trilobites had seventeen columns of lenses. So instead of gradual change, he said, he found stability, or stasis.

"If we chase fossil oysters up a cliff (going from older rocks to younger rocks)," Eldredge says, "we should see them slowly change before our eyes. Sometimes we do. More often . . . we do not."

An archaeologist prepares a skull of *Antrodemus* for scientific study.

As further proof of their idea of long periods of stability, Gould and Eldredge point out "living fossils" such as alligators and snapping turtles, horseshoe crabs and porcupines, that have not undergone evolutionary change in millions of years. They argue that certain species remain unchanged for a few million years and then disappear. Similar species may appear and survive for a shorter period, then disappear. In the meantime, other species simply appear. Evolution, says Gould, is "punctuated" with these macro-evolutionary events.

Stephen Gould and Niles Eldredge believe that animals that have remained unchanged for millions of years, such as the porcupine, support their theory of *punctuated equilibria*.

The pattern of punctuated equilibria is seen in human evolution, too, Eldredge writes in his book *The Myths of Human Evolution*. A good example of a stable, successful species is *Homo erectus*. *H. erectus* is midpoint in the trend toward increased brain size in humans. A study of fossils found from Eastern Africa to China shows that the brain size did not change significantly in *H. erectus*. There was only a slight increase in size at the time they became extinct. If Darwin's idea of slow, gradual change were true, Eldredge argues, *H. erectus* should have shown a gradual increase in brain size during their million years on earth. Also, he asks, if they were successful, why did they become extinct?

Evolution was not a slow, steady, gradual improvement or change through time, as Darwin saw it, Eldredge says. The observations of evolutionary biology show a picture of stability, with change difficult and rare.

Creationists

Ever since Darwin's book was published, people of many religions have rejected the Theory of Evolution. Today a group of such people have formed the Creationist Research Institute to investigate evolution for themselves.

Creationists believe there was no evolution. There was creation. One spokesperson for the Cre-

"The secrets of evolution are death and time—the deaths of enormous numbers of lifeforms that were imperfectly adapted to their environment; and time for a long succession of small mutations that were *by accident* adaptive, time for the slow accumulation of patterns of favorable mutations."

Dr. Carl Sagan, *Cosmos*

"Today the fossil record . . . is forcing us to revise this conventional view of evolution. . . . Major evolutionary transitions have been wrought during episodes of rapid change . . . evolution has moved by fits and starts."

Paleobiologist Steven M. Stanley, *The New Evolutionary Timetable*

ationist Research Institute, Duane T. Gish, explains it further in his book *Evolution? The Fossils Say No!*

"By creation," he writes, "we mean the bringing into being of the basic kinds of plants and animals by the process of sudden . . . creation described in the first two chapters of Genesis. Here we find the creation by God of the plants and animals, each commanded to reproduce after its own kind using processes which were essentially instantaneous. . . . During the creation week God created all of these basic animal and plant kinds, and since then no new kinds have come into being, for the Bible speaks of a *finished* creation (Gen. 2:2). . . . These facts directly contradict evolution theory."

The Bible as Truth

For Creationists, the "real truth of the matter" is found in the Bible. Henry Morris explains it further: "There is no scientific fallacy in the Bible at all. 'Science' is *knowledge,* and the Bible is a book of true and factual knowledge throughout, on every subject with which it deals. The Bible *is* a book of science!"

Creationists believe that Noah's flood is responsible for how the fossils were distributed in rocks. Perhaps, they say, denser and more streamlined objects descended more rapidly and populated the bottom strata (in conventional geology, the oldest strata). Or, species that lived on the ocean bottom were overcome by flood waters first and thus should lie in the lower strata. Those creatures that now are found on mountaintops somehow postponed their death and ended up in the upper strata. The third possibility is that certain animals with high intelligence or superior mobility might have struggled successfully for a time and ended up on top.

"The really crucial evidence for evolution must

be provided by the palaeontologist whose business it is to study the evidence of the fossil record," Gish says in his book.

Paleontologist Stephen Jay Gould believes science *has* found this evidence. He points out, "The geological record of fossils follows a single, invariant order throughout the world. The oldest rocks contain only single-celled creatures; invertebrates dominate lower strata, followed by the first fishes, then dinosaurs, and finally large mammals." If all creatures were created at once, he says, they would not have got sorted into that invariable order in earth's strata. The lower strata contains fossils of many delicate, floating creatures who were not dense enough to sink. Oceanic creatures—whales and certain fishes in particular—appear only in upper strata, well above many creatures who live on land. Clumsy sloths, who would not have superior mobility, are only found in strata lying well above scores of lithe and nimble small dinosaurs and pterosaurs.

"The very invariance of the universal fossil sequence," Gould says, "is the strongest argument" against a catastrophe such as a flood distributing the fossils among the rocks. "Surely," he says, "some-

A sloth hangs from a branch. The fossils of the sloth's ancestors are found only in strata above that of dinosaurs. Why are these animals found only in a particular strata? Does this mean that all creatures were not created at once?

A drawing depicts the creation of light, as described in the Book of Genesis.

where, at least one courageous trilobite would have paddled on valiantly (as its colleagues succumbed) and won a place in the upper strata. Surely, on some primordial beach, a [human] would have suffered a heart attack and been washed into the lower strata before intelligence had a chance to plot temporary escape."

How Did Evolution Happen?

Most scientists believe that life began with one organism in the primordial ocean billions of years ago and evolved either gradually or punctuationally into many varieties of species. But science cannot prove that. Science provides no more than a very high degree of certainty, says paleobiologist Steven M. Stanley in his book *New Evolutionary Timetable*. "One cannot prove, for instance, that the sun will appear in the east tomorrow. Throughout recorded history, it has shown in the east every morning. That means it almost certainly will make an appearance tomorrow, but we have no proof: we cannot generalize that the sun will *always* appear in the east."

But science can *disprove* something, Stanley goes on. Evolution has not only *not* been disproven, according to him, but it has gained strength. "Discovery of a horse fossil in Precambrian rocks could disprove evolution," he says. "Any topsy-turvy sequence of fossils would force science to rethink the theory, but as yet none has come to life."

Some things, though, back up scientific thinking about evolution. In the womb, for instance, as Gordon Rattray Taylor points out, both animals and humans go through what science sees as earlier phases of evolution. "For a few days," Taylor says, "the human embryo develops gills. A rudimentary tail is formed and occasionally persists until birth and after." Sara Stein in *The Evolution Book* adds, "Evolution is happening right now in unborn babies. The jawbone that is now the hinge on which your mouth swings open was separated from your skull by another small jawbone. As you developed, that small bone migrated upward to become the malleus, or hammer bone, of your middle ear. In moving from jaw to ear, the malleus in humans and other mammals repeats a migration that began 265 million years ago in the skulls of Therapsids (an early mammal)."

What also seems to back up evolution is something called *atavisms,* which are structures from the past. For instance, fossils have been found that show that the horse once had three toes. Today, horses are occasionally born with three toes. They are atavisms.

Creationists are not alone, though, in thinking that a Creator was involved. Alfred Russel Wallace, whose theory was made public when Darwin's was, believed that humans are a special creation. He believed that the human form evolved by natural selection, as other animals forms did. But he felt the scope and power of people's intellectual and moral nature suggests that "some other influence, law, or agency is required to account for them." He thought that a "superior intelligence had guided the development of man for a special purpose." He felt it was "utterly inconceivable that people's development as spiritual beings" resulted from natural selection.

Few, if any scientists believe in a six-day creation, as Creationists do. But Jeffrey Goodman and others believe, as Goodman says, "There is a definite sense of timing of evolution in the Old Testament. . . . Genesis depicts God's creation of life in general evolutionary stages—plants, fish, fowl, beasts, and finally man."

Could it be that a Creator is behind what Gordon Rattray Taylor sees as a "purposiveness" in evolution? Could the mechanics of evolution be the hand of God?

"If God made each of the half dozen human species discovered in ancient rocks, why did he create in an unbroken temporal sequence of progressively modern features—increasing cranial capacity, a reduced face and teeth, larger body size. Did he create to mimic evolution and test our faith thereby?"

Dr. Stephen Jay Gould, *Science and Creationism*

"The fossil-bearing strata were apparently laid down in large measure during the Flood, with apparent sequences attributed not to evolution but rather to hydrodynamic [shape and weight] selectivity, ecologic habitats, and differential mobility and strength of the various creatures."

Creation Scientist Dr. Henry M. Morris, *Scientific Creationism*

Four

A World of Chance or Purpose?

A hydra is a little animal about as big as the *I* of this type (about 1/8 inch long). It is not much more than a tube with a mouth at one end and a foot at the other. Arms waving around the mouth direct food into it. The foot attaches the hydra to underwater plants. The hydra moves by somersaulting. Some hydra develop stinging cells that contain a coiled poisoned hair. Another hair projects outside of the cell and works like a trigger. If something touches the outer hair, it releases the poisoned hair.

The planarian worm, another animal so small it can hardly be seen, sometimes eats hydra. The worm does not digest those special stinging cells, called *nematocysts*. Somehow, instead, it passes them through its body and positions them on its skin with the stinging points outward. Then, when enemies approach, it shoots the nematocysts like poisoned darts.

When the planarian worm is fully armed, it quits eating the hydra. After it has discharged its weapons, it "reloads" by eating hydra again.

Why the planarian worm eats hydra is one of the mysteries of evolution that cannot be explained by Darwin's theory, says Gordon Rattray Taylor in *The Great Evolution Mystery*. Physiologists, scien-

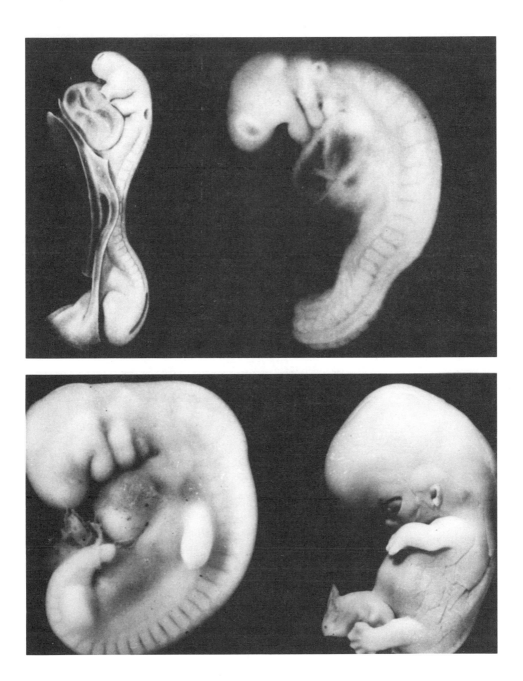

What accounts for the
seemingly limitless variety of
creatures on earth?

tists trained to understand how bodies work, cannot explain how the hydra migrate through the body of the planarian worm.

That migration, says Taylor, is similar to something else physiologists cannot explain: the migration of cells in an *embryo,* a baby in the early stages of development before birth. Why do cells from various places in the fertilized egg come together in one place to form the heart, as if they know their destiny is to become "heart" and nothing else, Taylor asks.

Taylor finds other things puzzling. "What," he asks, "is the explanation of the odd changes of tempo in evolution? In the last few million years [humans have] diverged dramatically from the original stock, while the other primates have changed much less. Other species, such as sharks and frogs, have hardly changed at all. In some lines, evolution seems to have stopped." Among mammals, he adds, several sequences appear to have started up simultaneously.

"It was not by chance that living things, in all their limitless variety, appeared upon this earth," Taylor says. The mystery of whether evolution happened by chance or as part of a grand design is one scientists continue to explore.

Did Living Things Appear by Chance?

Though he does not believe living things appeared by chance, Taylor also does not believe they came about through the workings of a "preconceived plan of divine origin." There have been far too many false starts and changes of intention for that. Extinctions are one thing that suggest evolution is not a thought out plan, Taylor says. It is estimated that 90 percent of all the species that have ever existed have become extinct. In addition, some land animals have gone back into the sea, some legged animals have become burrowers, and some birds have stopped flying. "Many forms," he adds, "which are regarded as successful variants—such as [humans]—turn out on examination to be very poorly designed. The prevalence of 'slipped discs' is one proof of that. Years ago, the Russian scientist Elie Metchnikoff remarked that he could point to at least 120 features of the human body which could have been much better designed by a good engineer." Why would a divine Creator have designed so imperfect a plan?

Taylor does not think that Darwin's theory of evolution explains the mystery of life either. He thinks that life itself "seeks new and subtler forms of expression by a blind impulse [driving force], and inner directedness."

Norman D. Newell, curator emeritus of the Amcrican Muscum of Natural History disagrees

"Darwin's ideas caused a furor when they were first announced because they presented the living world as a world of chance, determined by material forces, in place of a world determined by a divine plan. They substituted chance for purpose."

British television science advisor Gordon Rattray Taylor, *The Great Evolution Mystery*

"Part of our resistance to [the ideas of] Darwin and Wallace derives from our difficulty in imagining the passage of the millennia, much less the aeons. What does seventy million years mean to beings who live only one-millionth as long? We are like butterflies who flutter for a day and think it is forever."

Dr. Carl Sagan, *Cosmos*

with Taylor. Newell sees a *lack* of directedness in evolution. It leads him to conclude that evolution happened by chance. In his book *Creation and Evolution: Myth or Reality,* he says, "Since the sixteenth century, biologists have been trying to grapple with a steady stream of newly discovered organisms bought back from exploratory expeditions. The Scriptures had not prepared early naturalists for the many strange creatures that were brought to their attention!"

Why, he asks, did the Creator see fit to make so many local kinds of grazing animals? And why a different set of species for every major geographical region? In North America, he says, it was bison and pronghorn antelope, while Australia had more than a hundred species similar to kangaroos that were unknown elsewhere. The New World had more than three hundred species of hummingbirds, while Europe had none. Tiny organisms, *biota*, on the island of Madagascar are unlike those on the nearby African continent. The small community of plants and animals on Mount Ararat, where Noah's ark is said to have landed, look little like those of most other parts of the world. "The Genesis account did not harmonize at all with the facts of distribution of living organisms," he concluded. For Newell, science, not Scripture, presents an accurate picture.

But there are mysteries in the similarity of science's findings and incidents recorded in religious myths that puzzle other scientists and students of evolution. One mystery concerns the origin of life.

Origin of Life

How life began is probably the most tantalizing aspect of the theory of evolution.

In the Bible, the Book of Genesis says: "Then the Lord God formed man of dust from the ground."

In the Koran, the Book of Surah (chapter) 32:76

Why does Australia have so many species similar to the kangaroo?

says: "He began the creation of man from dust." (Some translations say *clay*.)

And after examining thousands of fossils and conducting laboratory experiments, scientists think it is in clay that the first primordial cell got its start.

One reason is that the clay molecule is almost identical to a hemoglobin molecule. It seems to scientists as though the clay molecule formed a "mold" for the hemoglobin molecule. Our blood is made up of hemoglobin molecules.

Another reason scientists think that life may have begun in clay is the structure of clay. It is formed of minute crystals and makes a good supporting structure for the building of difficult organic molecules, which is what make up human and other animal bodies and plants. Our bodies are made up of a hundred trillion cells. "We are each of us a multitude," says Carl Sagan in *Cosmos*.

North America has many species of bison corresponding to particular geographical locations. Why doesn't the Book of Genesis explain these variations?

A drop of blood seen through a microscope. The components of clay molecules are similar to those in hemoglobin—a respitory pigment in red blood cells. Did the clay molecule form a "mold" for the hemoglobin molecule?

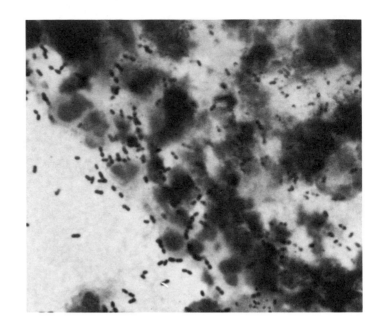

As small as a cell is, it is made up of something even smaller—molecules. "Every cell in your body is a kind of commune," Sagan says, "with once free-living parts all banded together for the common good." The cells in a drop of blood contain a "sort of molecular factory, the *mitochondrion,* which combines food with oxygen to extract useful energy. . . . Today's white blood cell was yesterday's creamed spinach."

Some scientists think that all those molecules that make up a cell first got their start in clay. The basic ingredients for organic molecules—atoms—were in the poisonous air that first filled earth's atmosphere. Those ingredients were mostly carbon, along with nitrogen, hydrogen, and sulfur. "Other necessary elements became available," explains Sara Stein in *The Evolution Book,* "as rain dissolved them from the [earth's] crust and deposited them in the form of clay." One of the elements clay provided is *kaolinite,* which is an ingredient in Kaopectate, a medication used to relieve diarrhea. Kaolinite makes things "stick together."

Clay had another special quality, according to scientist A.G. Cairns-Smith. Clay is made up of minute crystals that Cairns-Smith thinks provided a scaffold-like form within which smaller molecules could be held in position for assembly into larger ones. Cairns-Smith thinks that the molecules produced by clay evolved with it.

"If that is so," says Sara Stein, author of *The Evolution Book,* "there is truth in what religion tells us: Life came from clay."

A Hopi Myth

Religious traditions explaining other mysteries of evolution also seem to be borne out by science.

For Jeffrey Goodman, anthropologist and geologist, "a myth comes to life" as he examines and oversees excavations in the southwestern United States. The myth is a Hopi Indian creation story which says that three worlds existed prior to the one in which people now live.

During the first world, the Hopis say, their ancestors were highly advanced; they had domesticated corn and animals. The first world was eventually destroyed by fire because the people turned away from the gods' teachings. The second world was created to give the people another chance. Again, because the people strayed from the teachings, the second world was destroyed, this time by ice. A third world was created and again was destroyed, by water.

"To the Hopi," Goodman says in his book *American Genesis,*

> these worlds existed in the San Francisco mountains . . . outside of Flagstaff, Arizona. These worlds . . . make geologic sense. The destruction of the Hopi's third world by water may correspond to the inner-mountain basin damming and flooding that took place approximately 25,000 years ago in the Flagstaff mountains. The destruction of the

"If one wishes to believe that the universe and everything in it were created by a supreme being, there is nothing in the theory of evolution to contradict that."

Science editor Dennis Flanagan, *Flanagan's Version*

"Evolution is not the execution of a consummate overall plan, divine or otherwise. There have been far too many false starts, boss shots and changes of intentions for that. The human body could have been much better designed by a good engineer."

British television science advisor Gordon Rattray Taylor, *The Great Evolution Mystery*

"As we look out into the universe and identify the many accidents of physics and astronomy that have worked together for our benefit, it almost seems as if the universe must in some sense have known that we were coming."

Physicist Freeman Dyson, *Omni Interviews*

"Occasionally someone remarks on what a lucky coincidence it is that the Earth is perfectly suitable for life. . . . But this is, in part, a confusion of cause and effect. We earthlings are supremely well adapted to the environment of the Earth because we grew up here."

Dr. Carl Sagan, *Cosmos*

second world by ice could represent the glacial activity that took place in the peaks approximately 100,000 years ago. And the destruction of the first world by fire could represent the volcanic activity that took place in the mountains approximately 250,000 years ago. A recent archaeological discovery in the area gives added support to Hopi myth. At this dig I have discovered the oldest known geometrically engraved stone in the world, an engraving two to three times as old as similar engravings made by Cro-Magnon. . . . Thus, as with the story of creation and the flood in the Bible, the basic elements and sequence of Hopi legend could be correct.

Goodman goes on to say that when some early archeologists followed clues gleaned from Hopi and Zuni myths, they found archaeological sites rich with "finds."

Role of a Creator

In another of his books, *The Genesis Mystery,* Goodman explores the idea of the possible role of a Creator in evolution. "What *was* the true origin of mankind?" he asks. "While the theory of evolution effectively explains the development of the animal kingdom and even of 'near men,' it is not the only possible scientific theory to explain the appearance of fully modern man [Homo sapiens sapiens]. . . . Physically and mentally he took a great leap beyond his predecessors, a leap which cannot be explained by the demands of the environment or random mutation."

He quotes other scientists to support his argument. Alfred Russel Wallace's theory of evolution, which was announced at the same time as Darwin's, differed in one point. Wallace agreed that modern human body structure probably evolved from "the lower animals" through natural selection. But he believed "the unseen universe of Spirit" accounted for human intellectual and moral aspects. Wallace

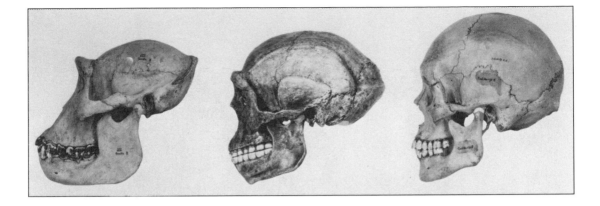

believed that a "superior intelligence" had guided human development.

Frederick Soddy, according to Goodman, saw evolution in a different light. Soddy won a Nobel prize in 1921 for his scientific work. He wondered if it was because of the fall of man spoken of in Genesis that the world was "plunged back" under the control of nature, "to begin once more its upward toilsome journey through the ages."

Sir John Eccles received a Nobel prize for his work on nerve synapses in the brain. Eccles said the human self survives beyond the death of the physical brain. He stated, "If I say that the uniqueness of the human self is not derived from the genetic code, not derived from experience, then what is it derived from? My answer is this: from a divine creation. Each self is a divine creation."

"The gaps between modern man and his predecessors," Goodman says, "are so profound that something more than random gene flow and natural selection may well be involved. How could the many highly coordinated characteristics of man have come together at random? The odds are beyond imagination."

Owen Gingerich, professor of Astronomy and of History of Science at Harvard University, sees what he calls "the designer's hand" at work in the

From left to right are the skulls of a gorilla, a prehistoric man, and a modern man. Does natural selection account for the differences between modern man and his predecessors?

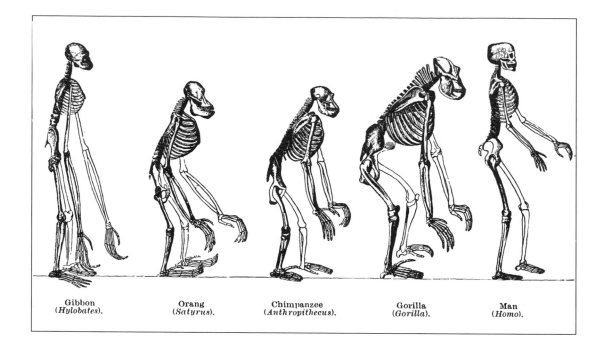

Gibbon
(*Hylobates*).

Orang
(*Satyrus*).

Chimpanzee
(*Anthropithecus*).

Gorilla
(*Gorilla*).

Man
(*Homo*).

Does this chart from the book *Evolution of Man* represent millions of years of evolution?

"small marvels" of evolution. "In the microscopic world, there are marvels that stagger the imagination," he says. One of those marvels is the way in which the carbon atom works.

The Hand of God

Carbon is essential to the chemical basis of all life on earth. But carbon is not very abundant, Gingerich says. There are 250 helium atoms for every carbon atom. A carbon nucleus can be made by mergine three helium atoms, but such a triple collision is rare. Once three helium atoms do collide, though, the internal workings of the carbon nucleus helps the process along. "It turns out," says Gingerich, "that there is precisely the right resonance within the carbon that helps this process along. Without it, there would be relatively few carbon atoms. . . . Had the carbon resonance been 4 percent higher, there would be essentially no carbon. . . . Without that carbon abundance, neither you nor I would be here."

Gingerich looks at the scientific worldview as a grand tapestry.

> It is an interlocked and coherent picture, a most workable explanation, but it is not the ultimate truth. . . . Perhaps the ultimate truth is that the world was created only 6,000 years ago, but since the Creator has filled it with wonderful clues pointing back 10 or 20 billion years, I am content to do my science by building a coherent picture of a multibillion-year-old creation. . . . Because it is the coherency of the picture and the systematic procedures for getting there—not the final truth—that science is all about.

"Are there valid scientific reasons for believing in [divine] creation?" asks Kenneth R. Miller. "Some respectable scientists clearly think so. Chandra Wickramasinghe and Fred Hoyle have argued as much in recent years. They have concluded that the ten or fifteen-billion-year-age suggested for the universe does not allow enough time for evolu-

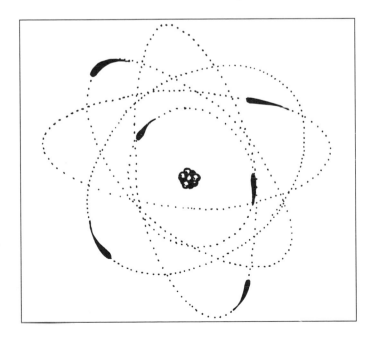

The carbon atom is essential to all life. This chemical element is found in all organic compounds.

86

"Darwin neglected to argue that, at least metaphorically, Genesis depicts God's creation of life in general evolutionary stages—plants, fish, fowl, beasts and finally man. There is a definite sense of timing, of evolution in the Old Testament."

Archeologist and geologist Jeffrey Goodman, *The Genesis Mystery*

"The world is ordered, but the order springs from an inner necessity. Chance is restricted. As time passes, the number of possibilities becomes fewer. Like a steel ball rolling down a pin ball machine, the nearer we get to our destination, the more limited the possible outcome becomes."

British television science advisor Gordon Rattray Taylor, *The Great Evolution Mystery*

tion of the genetic codes found in living cells." Wickramasinghe goes even farther, Miller reports. He says that to say life can evolve from inanimate matter is like saying "a tornado sweeping through a junkyard might assemble a Boeing 747."

Not in the Realm of Science

The scientists who feel a Creator was involved in evolution generally keep their religious feelings separate from their science.

"Science simply does not deal with divinities," says paleobiologist Steven Stanley in his book *The New Evolutionary Timetable*.

> Observations and measurements are the raw material of science. Revelations, both personal and spiritual, and faith are the raw materials of religion. . . . Scientists may be religious—and many evolutionists are—and yet their religious views. . . cannot legitimately impinge upon science. . . . I have no idea whether Neanderthal had a soul or not, but he thought he did! This, anthropology tells us with a high degree of certainty. We have found Neanderthal burial sites that tell anthropologists that they revered their dead.

Stanley says Charles Darwin's theory that evolution occurs by natural selection, by blind chance, horrified people who had once seen the hand of God involved in creation. But, according to anybody who has read Darwin's letters, he did not see his theory as being "against God." He continued to believe in God, but he saw God working through natural law.

The problem with Creationists, say Stanley and other scientists, is that they do not look for answers. They tend to view anything not explainable as "that's God's choice." Whereas, science, Stanley says, "is compelled by its very nature" to look for objective, provable answers.

The mystery of whether a Creator was involved in evolution may never be unraveled. But how evolution works continues to tantalize scientists, whatever their religious beliefs. Much more is known about evolution since Darwin first shocked the world with his theory. Some of the mysteries that puzzled Darwin and other scientists of his day have been solved. What mysteries are scientists focusing on today? How are they trying to solve them? Is evolution still happening?

Five

What Mysteries Are Scientists Exploring Now?

(Opposite page) A full metamorphosis must be undergone before this tadpole reaches adulthood. In some ways, the transformation from tadpole to frog is similar to the processes of evolution.

One mystery of evolution can be seen at small ponds where frogs gather. The mystery is *metamorphosis,* the changing from one form into another. It can be seen when a tadpole turns into a frog. Within a week or so, an animal that lives in water, "breathing" water, eating plant fragments, and swimming by means of a powerful tail, becomes transformed into a four-legged animal, living on land, breathing air, and eating insects (meat). The thin, permeable, breathing skin of the tadpole becomes the thick, impermeable skin of the frog.

Other changes occur that cannot be seen. The tadpole excretes ammonia, like fish, which is diluted by the surrounding water. The frog cannot afford to do this. It would be poisoned. It excretes urea (from which the name urine comes). The tadpole's blood also changes, and the enzymes used to digest food change.

"The changes are exquisitely timed," says Gordon Rattray Taylor. "The tail does not begin to vanish until legs are ready. The gills do not resorb until the air-pumping mechanism is functional."

Watching a tadpole become a frog is like seeing evolutionary history at work, when fish became amphibians. But how does it happen?

A butterfly emerges from its cocoon. Scientists are baffled by the striking metamorphosis of these insects.

The metamorphosis of insects like the butterfly is even more striking. Not only is the larva very different in appearance from the butterfly, but many more structural changes occur in the metamorphosis. The changes involve nerves, muscles, gut, the reproductive organs, the respiratory system, circulation, fat bodies, skin, the alimentary canal, and so on. "In fact," says scientist John Whitten from Northwestern University, "there would appear . . . to be no system [in the butterfly] that remains unaffected by the metamorphic changes."

Even stranger, for Taylor, is the case of the red eft, which is a variety of newt. The red eft comes out of the water and spends three years on land. As it comes out of the water, it loses its *lateral line,* an organ peculiar to fish. It gains the kind of tongue useful for catching insects. After three years, it returns to water. "Then it metamorphoses back again," says Taylor, "losing its tongue and regaining its lateral line. It is evident that the genes for forming the lateral line were not lost, only supressed." Why it metamorphoses at all is an evolutionary mystery some scientists are trying to solve. One day, perhaps, the science of genetics may unravel the mystery.

New Discoveries

Genetics is one of a number of new sciences that have come into being because scientists want to solve some of the mysteries of evolution that puzzled Darwin and other early scientists.

With the first discovery of genetics, scientists began to understand how the random changes Darwin saw occurring in evolution happened. The combination and recombination (mixing up) and mutations of genes enable organisms to change and evolve. Genetics helped scientists understand how the variability of evolution happened, why there are such different and so many kinds of life.

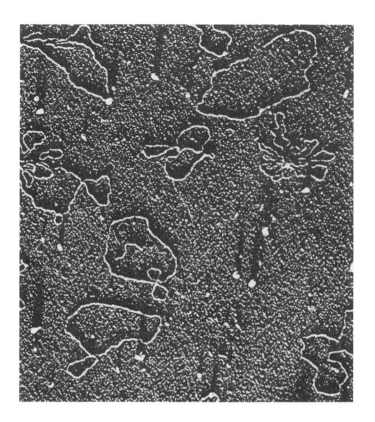

A greatly enlarged photo shows the strings of DNA. The strings join together in different patterns to form the genetic code, or set of instructions for the genes.

But modern knowledge of genetics also poses new mysteries. Why, for instance, are there so many different blood groups among humans? Although through the working of genetics one can understand *how* these blood groups could come into being, geneticist Richard Lewontin says, *why* they did is "utterly mysterious." Lewontin and other scientists are investigating the mystery of why natural selection has not eliminated all but the most efficient of the blood types.

Murray Eden is professor of genetic engineering at the Massachusetts Institute of Technology. He asks whether mutations and random chance really account for evolutionary changes. If it takes six mutations to bring about adaptive change, Murray says, such change would occur by chance only once

92

"I don't think humanity is going to be a single species much longer—maybe because of divergent evolution as we expand into space, and maybe sooner than that via genetic manipulation . . . people are going to want to make their children better than themselves, and the techniques to do that will be available in the next century."

Physicist Freeman Dyson, *Omni Interviews*

"Provided we can survive the complications of war, environmental degradation, and possible contact with interstellar planetary travelers, we will [in a few million years] look exactly as we do now. We will grow bigger because of better food, but there are not going to be any new physical adaptations. . . . If we survive, we will survive unchanged."

Paleontologist Richard Leakey, *Omni Interviews*

in a billion years. If two dozen mutations are involved, it would require ten billion years, which is longer than the earth is old. There has not been enough time for all the changes of evolution to have happened. Something more than chance mutation must occur, he concludes. The mystery is, what? Right now, the answer is not known, but molecular biology is carrying the study of genetics even farther.

Genetic Code

One area of research in molecular biology has been DNA, deoxyribonucleic (pronounced *dee-oxie-rye-bow-nu-clay-ic*) acid. DNA is the master molecule that contains the genetic code. It tells the genes what to do. DNA is made up of a string of units called nucleotides, which come in four varieties. They are called A, C, G, and T, from the initials of the letters of the substances of which they are made. Like the letters of the alphabet, those nucleotides join together in different ways to create different "sentences" of instructions for the genes. Gordon Rattray Taylor gives an example of how changes or omissions might affect a DNA "sentence": The sentence, *The cat sat on the mat* could become *The rat sat on the hat* with only two substitutions in the code. By adding a letter the original sentence could become *The cat spat on the mat*. Likewise, adding a nucleotide to a DNA sentence would cause a genetic change or mutation.

As a result of the discovery of how DNA works, science took a giant step forward. Further molecular research has shown that many more possibilities of mutations are possible than it was first thought, thus making the evolution mystery even more complicated.

A typical bacterium, like a germ, contains about three million nucleotides which code about three thousand genes. A mammalian cell (like that in hu-

mans) seems to have eight hundred times more DNA than a bacterium, but the amphibian toad has many more than that. The organism with the most DNA of those studied thus far, says Taylor, is the lily. It can have from ten thousand to one hundred thousand more than a bacterium.

Measuring DNA is complicated, though, because some animals have redundant DNA, or extra duplicates. This redundant DNA is not used. Why does it happen? What is its function? These are mysteries yet to be solved. One suggestion is that redundant DNA might be made up of mutant forms which the cell is waiting to try out or get rid of. Would that explain how random change can occur faster than Murray Eden worked out? More study and experiments may provide the answer.

Creating Life in the Lab

Scientists continue to conjecture about how life began, and they try to duplicate the process. In laboratory experiments, the building blocks of

The lily has the most DNA of any organism studied thus far.

life—amino acids—have been created. Harold Urey and Stanley Miller won a Nobel prize for the first such experiment in the 1950s.

Figuring that the early atmosphere was rich in hydrogen, they mixed hydrogen with methane and ammonia gases in a flask, recreating what they thought made up the earth's early atmosphere and oceans. They added electric sparks to simulate lightning. When they examined the water in the flask, they found that some basic organic chemicals, including some of the amino acids, had been created. The thick mixture of organic molecules left in the flask has come to be called *primordial soup*. From that experiment, scientists believe that the ocean on the young earth was primordial soup.

Many scientists think that life arose spontaneously in that rich environment. But scientists

Scientists believe that the ocean of prehistoric times was a kind of primordial soup—a rich mixture of organic molecules from which life spontaneously arose.

have not been able to prove it. They have not been able to create life itself. One scientist who wants to create life in the laboratory is Cyril Ponnamperuma, professor of chemistry and director of the Laboratory of Chemical Evolution at the University of Maryland. "We are looking for an orderly sequence, from atoms to small molecules to large molecules to replicating systems," from the beginnings of the universe eighteen billion to twenty billion years ago to the time the first man walked on earth. Ponnamperuma is talking about chemical evolution.

The "warm little pond," which Darwin first suggested might be where life began, says Ponnamperuma, "has in it the entire concept of chemical evolution. What we try to do in the laboratory is to recreate Darwin's warm little pond." Ponnamperuma's office reflects his work. On a shelf stands a Campbells' soup can, relabeled *Primordial Soup*. A picture on the wall shows well-known chef Julia Child stirring one of his smelly organic concoctions.

Through his experiments, Ponnamperuma is trying to show that basic—or primordial— molecules would have combined to form larger protein and nucleic molecules that could duplicate themselves. Nucleic acids are the building blocks of genes. "If we can create such molecules," he says, "we will have created the genetic code. If we can create the genetic code, we will have created life itself."

Life from Outer Space

Thus far, scientists studying chemical evolution have not created life. But through their research they have learned that the genetic code is essentially the same throughout the universe. "We study meteorites," Ponnamperuma says, searching for evidence of life and clues to its source. Meteorites are small pieces of rock from the asteroid belt that get trapped in the earth's gravitational field and fall to

"Theories, or statements about the causes of documented evolutionary change, are now in a period of intense debate—a good mark of science in its healthiest state."

Dr. Stephen Jay Gould, *Discover* Magazine, January 1987

"The Creator . . . *used processes which are not now operating anywhere in the natural universe.* . . . We cannot discover by scientific investigations anything about the creative processes."

Creation scientist Dr. Duane T. Gish, *Evolution? The Fossils Say No!*

A meteorite shoots across the sky. Scientists analyze the physical composition of meteorites to learn about life throughout the universe.

the ground. Through analysis of meteorites scientists have been able to establish evidence that amino acids were forming even before the planets were born, Ponnamperuma says. Research in outer space by radio-astronomers has identified more than fifty-three other organic molecules—from which proteins and nucleic acids can be made. From such evidence, Ponnamperuma and other scientists conclude there is other life in the universe.

"There are 10^{23} possibilities [that is ten, followed by twenty-three zeros] for life," Ponnamperuma says, "because there are 10^{23} stars in the universe." Even if only 5 percent of them have all the conditions suitable to life, he says, it is still a very big number.

Francis Crick, one of the discoverers of the double-helix structure of DNA, suggests that life may have existed in outer space even before it existed on earth. He theorizes that the seeds of life were sent here by "creatures like ourselves." After the seeds were deposited in the primordial soup, they evolved as the fossil record indicates. He admits that his idea, called *panspermia*—the seeding of life—"stinks of science fiction." But he thinks the chance of life evolving through a natural sequence or events of earth is improbable. He, too, believes there is life elsewhere in the universe, which was also seeded by this other civilization. That life might not be life as we know it. It would depend, he says, on how it evolved.

The mystery of how or where life began continues to intrigue scientists, and they search for the answer.

Epilogue

The Search Goes On

(Opposite page) Charles
Darwin ponders the
evolutionary question. What
accounts for the diversity
and adaptedness of living
creatures?

Evolution is happening right now, but it is so gradual the human eye cannot see it. The Atlantic Ocean is getting bigger. Each year it is growing about the same amount a person's fingernails grow in a year. In East Africa, the ground is opening up. In a million, maybe ten million years, there might be an ocean in the Great Rift Valley of East Africa. The Himalayan Mountains and the Alps are growing taller. In ten million years, Los Angeles may be sitting right next to San Francisco. Five hundred million years from now the earth and its creatures may look as different as they did five hundred million years ago.

Researching the earth's movements is possible because new scientific equipment has been invented that can tell people things that once were unknown. In Darwin's day, research "apparatus" for the study of evolution consisted mainly of sharp eyes and notebooks in which to record observations. Today, larger and more complicated telescopes and space vehicles provide better pictures of what is happening in the universe. More powerful microscopes allow scientists to study tiny remnants from the past such as the blue-green algae fossil that, magnified one to two thousand times, is smaller

than a dime. All of these new tools and more may help scientists unravel the mysteries of evolution.

Humans will continue to search for the answers. The ancient lights in the sky will continue to pique human curiosity but today people will explore them with sophisticated instruments. The apparatus of science may change, but the yearning to know does not.

"The excitement of the chase is properly our quarry," said the sixteenth-century French essayist Montaigne. "We are born to search after the truth."

And so the search for answers to the mysteries of evolution goes on.

(Opposite page) Evolution is a continuing process. With advancing technology and more sophisticated instruments, such as the telescope shown here, man will continue to search for the answers to the riddle.

Glossary

ancestor   the organism or type of organism from which later organisms evolved.

biota   animal and plant life.

cosmos   the Universe regarded as a systematically arranged whole; an orderly, harmonious system.

embryo   an organism in its early developmental stage, or before birth.

embryonic   related to early developmental stage.

evolution   a gradual process of change or development; the theory that existing species of plants and animals have developed from previously existing plants and animals through a process of gradual change.

fauna   animals as a group, as: The fauna of North America.

flora   plants as a group.

hominid   a scientific term for classification of human-like beings.

macro-evolution   a scientific term for major evolutionary change, as when fish evolved into amphibians (creatures who live in both water and on land, such as crocodiles).

metamorphosis   a change in appearance, condition, structure. Used in biology to indicate change in structure and habits of an animal during growth.

micro-evolution   a scientific term for small evolutionary change, such as when the shape of a bird's beak changes.

notocord   a backbone-like structure, but it has no separate vertebra as backbones do.

opposable   in a contrasting position, such as position of the human thumb in relation to fingers, which allows thumb and finger to come together to pick up even very small objects.

organism   a scientific term meaning a living being, such as a plant or animal.

photosynthesis   the process by which plants use sunlight to convert carbon dioxide and water into carbohydrates (sugar food). The waste left over in the process is oxygen, which the plants release into the air.

primates   a scientific term for a group of mammals (animals who nurse their young), that includes monkeys, apes, and humans.

primordial   a term scientists use to describe the era when the earth was first formed. A term to describe something in its original state.

primordial soup   a term scientists use to describe ocean water that was thick with such chemical elements as hydrogen, oxygen, nitrogen, carbon, etc.

punctuated equilibria   a theory of evolution that says life remained much the same for long periods of time, then was punctuated with major evolutionary changes, such as when fish fins evolved into legs.

saltation   a jump, as when a major evolutionary change was made.

speciation   the formation of two (or more) new species from a single existing species; when an existing species evolves into two or more new species.

species   a scientific term used to describe plants or animals of a kind; plants or animals who can reproduce young who can also produce young.

stasis   a state of balance; a state, for instance, when things do not change.

static   not in motion, at rest.

tectonic plates   large pieces of the earth's crust that move. The earth's surface, which appears solid, is made up of seven large tectonic plates and twenty smaller ones.

For Further Exploration

Michael Benton, *The Story of Life on Earth,* New York and London: Warwick Press, 1986.

Barbara Cork and Lynn Bresler, *Young Scientist Book of Evolution,* London: Usborne Publishing, Ltd., 1985.

Jon Erickson, *Volcanoes and Earthquakes,* Summit Ridge, PA: TAB Books, 1988.

Eyewitness Book: *Early Humans,* New York: Alfred Knopf, 1989.

Roy A. Gallant, *Charles Darwin: The Making of a Scientist,* New York: Doubleday, 1972.

Roy A. Gallant, *Fossils,* New York: Franklin Watts, 1985.

Arthur S. Gregor, *The Adventure of Man,* New York: Macmillan, 1966.

Kim Marshall, *The Story of Life, from the Big Bang to You,* New York: Holt, Rinehard and Winston, 1980.

Ruth Moore, *Life* editors, *Evolution,* A Time/Life book, New York: Time, Inc., 1962.

Sara Stein, *The Evolution Book,* New York: Workman Publishing, 1986.

Magazine articles:

"Extinction," *National Geographic,* June 1989.

Works Consulted

Joanne Abrams, ed., *Evolution: New Perspectives.* Mosaic Reader Series. Wayne, NJ: Avery Publishing Group, 1983.

Gene Bylinsky, *Life in Darwin's Universe.* Garden City. NY: Doubleday & Co., Inc., 1981.

Maitland A. Edey and Donald C. Johanson, *Blueprints: Solving the Mystery of Evolution.* Boston: Little, Brown and Co., 1989.

Maitland A. Edey and Donald C. Johanson, *Lucy: The Beginnings of Humankind.* New York: Simon and Schuster, 1981.

Don L. Eicher, A. Lee McAlester and Marcia L. Rottman, *The History of the Earth's Crust.* Englewood, NJ: Prentice-Hall, 1984.

Niles Eldredge, *Time Frames.* New York: Simon and Schuster, 1985.

Niles Eldredge and Ian Tattersall, *The Myths of Human Evolution.* New York: Columbia University Press, 1982.

Penelope Farmer, *Beginnings: Creation Myths of the World.* New York: Atheneum, 1979.

Dennis Flanagan, *Flanagan's Version: A Spectator's Guide to Science on the Eve of the 21st Century.* New

York: Alfred A. Knopf, 1988.

Roland Mushat Frey, ed., *Is God a Creationist?*. New York: Charles Scribner's Sons, 1981.

Laurie R. Godfrey, *Scientists Confront Creationism*. New York: W.W. Norton, 1983.

Jeffrey Goodman, *American Genesis*. New York: Summit Books, 1981. *Genesis Mystery*. New York: Times Books, 1983.

Human Evolution. Mosaic Reader Series. Wayne, NJ: Avery Publishing Group, 1983.

Robert Jastrow, *Enchanted Loom: Mind in the Universe*. New York: Simon and Schuster, 1981.

Philip Kitcher, *Abusing Science. The Case Against Creationism*. Cambridge, MA: MIT Press, 1982.

A. Lee McAlester, *The History of Life*. Englewood, NJ: Prentice-Hall, 1977.

David Maclagan, *Creation Myths*. London: Thames and Hudson Publishers, 1977.

Ashley Montagu, ed., *Science and Creationism*. Oxford, England: Oxford University Press, 1984.

Henry M. Morris, *Scientific Creationism*. San Diego, CA: Creation-Life Publishers, 1978.

John Napier, *The Origins of Man*. New York: McGraw-Hill, 1968.

Norman D. Newell, *Creation and Evolution*. New York: Columbia University Press, 1982.

Barry Parker, *Creation: The Story of the Origin and Evolution of the Universe*. New York: Plenum Press, 1988.

John Reader, *Missing Links: The Hunt for Earliest Man*. Boston: Little, Brown and Co., 1981.

Carl Sagan, *Cosmos*. New York: Random House, 1980.

Carl Sagan, *Dragons of Eden*. New York: Bantam Books, 1977.

Steven M. Stanley, *The New Evolutionary Timetable*. New York: Basic Books, Inc., 1981.

Gordon Rattray Taylor, *The Great Evolution Mystery*. New York: Harper and Row Publishers 1983, 1983.

Howard J. Van Till, *The Fourth Day*. Grand Rapids, MI: Wm. B. Eerdmans Publishing Col, 1986.

Pamela Weintraub, *Omni Interviews*. New York: Ticknor & Fields, 1984.

Magazine articles:

"Darwinism Defined: The Difference Between Fact and Theory," *Discover*. January 1987.

Index

About the Author

Marilyn L. Bailey has worked as a newspaper journalist (where she won an award for her work); as a magazine editor and staff writer; and as a freelance writer. She has written more than a thousand articles and short stories for both adults and children. One of her children's stories was recently chosen to be included in an anthology. She is an instructor of writing for children. This is her third book for young people.

She loves mystery and history and enjoys digging for information with the investigative research skills she learned as a journalist.

A mother of four grown children, she lives in a suburb of St. Paul, Minnesota.

Picture Credits